A TEXTBOOK ON
BUSINESS LAWS

A TEXTBOOK ON
BUSINESS LAWS

Dr. Anita Soni
M.Com, MBA (Ex.), Ph.D. UGC NET

Dr. Meenu
M.Com, Ph.D, UGC NET & JRF

REGAL PUBLICATIONS
New Delhi - 110 027

A TEXTBOOK ON BUSINESS LAWS

ISBN 978-81-8484-591-4 [PB]

Typeset by
THE LASER PRINTERS
8/15, 3rd Floor, Subhash Nagar, New Delhi-110027

Printed in India at
NEW ELEGANT PRINTERS
A-49/1, Mayapuri Phase-I, New Delhi-110064

Published by
REGAL PUBLICATIONS
F-159, Rajouri Garden, New Delhi-110027
Phones : 45546396, 25435369
E-mail : regalbookspub@yahoo.com, regaldeepbooks@yahoo.com

CONTENTS

Preface ix

Syllabus xi

UNIT - I

1. Negotiable Instruments **1**

- 1.1 Introduction 1
- 1.2 Definition of Negotiable Instrument 2
- 1.3 Essential Characteristics of Negotiable Instruments 3
- 1.4 Types of Negotiable Instruments 4
- 1.5 Conclusion 7

2. Promissory Note, Bills of Exchange and Cheque **9**

- 2.1 Introduction 10
- 2.2 Essential features of a Promissory Note 11
- 2.3 Bill of Exchange 12
- 2.4 Essential Features of a Bill of Exchange 12
- 2.5 The Procedure for Transfer a Bill of Exchange 13
- 2.6 Cheque 14
- 2.7 Essential Features of a Cheque 14
- 2.8 Difference Between Bill of Exchange and Promissory Note 15
- 2.9 Dishonour of Cheques 17
- 2.10 Distinguishing Features of Cheques, Bill of Exchange and Promissory Note 18
- 2.11 Difference Between a Cheque and a Bill of Exchange 22
- 2.12 Other Types of Negotiable Instruments 24
- 2.13 Rules Regarding Accommodation Bills 25
- 2.14 Conclusion 26

3. **Parties to Negotiable Instruments** 30
3.1 Parties to Negotiable Instruments 30
3.2 Liability of Parties 32
3.3 Holder and Holder in Due Course 36
3.4 Privileges of Holder in Due Course 38
3.5 Difference between Holder and Holder in Due Course 41
3.6 Holder for Value 41
3.7 Payment in Due Course 41
3.8 Conclusion 42

4. **Discharge of Parties from Liability** 47
4.1 Meaning of "Discharge" 47
4.2 Discharge of Negotiable Instruments 48
4.3 Discharge of Party Secondarily Liable (Sec. 112) 49
4.4 Discharge of Parties from Liability 51
4.5 Discharge by Operation of Law (Sec. 120) 52
4.6 Discharge by Operation of Law is not Included 52
4.7 Conclusion 52

5. **Dishonour of Negotiable Instrument** 57
5.1 Introduction 57
5.2 Dishonour of Negotiable Instrument 58
5.3 Effect of Dishonour 58
5.4 Consequences of not giving Notice of Dishonour 60
5.5 Conclusion 65

6. **Negotiation and Endorsement** 67
6.1 Introduction—Negotiation 67
6.2 Modes of Negotiation 68
6.3 Assignment 68
6.4 Endorsement 69
6.5 Negotiation Back 74
6.6 Conclusion 78

7. **The Information Technology Act, 2008** 84
7.1 Introduction 84
7.2 Definitions 86
7.3 Digital Signature 88
7.4 Electronic Governance 89
7.5 Attribution, Acknowledgment and Despatch of Electronic Records 91
7.6 Secure Electronic Records and Secure Digital Signatures 93
7.7 Regulation of Certifying Authorities 94
7.8 Digital Signature Certificates 100

7.9 Duties of Subscribers 102
7.10 Penalties and Adjudication 104
7.11 The Cyber Regulations Appellate Tribunal 106
7.12 Technical Aspects 106
7.13 Offences 108
7.14 Prevention of Fraud 109

UNIT - II

8. Consumer Protection Act, 1986 112
8.1 Introduction 112
8.2 Consumer Protection Act, 1986 113
8.3 Consumer Rights 113
8.4 Definitions 114
8.5 Consumer Protection Councils 122
8.6 Consumer Disputes Redressal Agencies 124
8.7 Composition of the District Forum 125
8.8 Composition of the State Commission 131
8.9 Composition of the National Commission 136
8.10 Appeal 140
8.11 Penalties 142
8.12 Miscellaneous 143
8.13 Conclusion 146

9. The Environment (Protection) Act, 1986 149
9.1 Definitions 150
9.2 Objective and Scope of the Environment (Protection) Act, 1986 151
9.3 Powers Provided by the Act to Central Government 152
9.4 Appointment of Officers and their Powers and Function 154
9.5 Power to give Directions 154
9.6 Rules to Regulate Environmental Pollution 155
9.7 Prevention, Control, and Abatement of Environmental Pollution 155
9.8 Persons Handling Hazardous Substances to Comply with Procedural Safeguards 156
9.9 Furnishing of Information to Authorities and Agencies in Certain Cases 156
9.10 Powers of Entry and Inspection 156
9.11 Power to take Sample and Procedure to be followed in Connection Therewith 158
9.12 Environmental Laboratories 159
9.13 Government Analysts 159
9.14 Reports of Government Analysts 159

Act and the Rules, Orders and Directions 160
9.16 Offences by Companies 160
9.17 Offences by Government Departments 161
9.18 Conclusion 161

10. Right to Information Act, 2005 163
10.1 Introduction 163
10.2 Definitions 164
10.3 Scope and Extent 169
10.4 Right to Information and Obligations of Public Authorities 169
10.5 Powers and Functions of the Information Commissions, Appeal and Penalties 174
10.6 Conclusion 178

Bibliography 180

Index 182

PREFACE

We are highly pleased to place in the hands of esteemed readers the first edition of our book "Business Laws" especially designed for the B.Com students. The students of BBA, B.Com. M.Com and MBA of Panjab University, Punjabi University, IGNOU, PTU and GNDU also have enough to pick out of it. All efforts have been made to simplify the concepts for instant understanding of students.

Our aim is to provide students with a textbook that is up to date and comprehensive in its coverage of legal and regulatory issues and obliged to enable instructors to tailor the materials to their specific approach. This book also engages students by relating laws to everyday events with which they are already familiar (or which they are familiarizing themselves in other business courses) by its clear, concise and readable style.

The book has been brought directly in line with the amended Business Law syllabus of B.Com. Therefore the book provides marketing students with a thorough working knowledge of the law on contract, sale of goods, agency, as well as the legal mechanisms for resolving commercial disputes, together with coverage of other selected topics which are of paramount importance to marketeers and businessmen in general. Business Law offers comprehensive coverage of the key aspects which are easy to understand for both law and non-law students.

We owe our gratitude to the distinguished authors who have been referred to at many places in this book.

We express our heartiest gratitude to Sr. Nirmal Singh, Chairman, Punjab Group of Colleges, Chunni Kalan, Fatehgarh Sahib for his support during the work.

Special thanks to Mr. Aman Sharma and Manjot Kaur, Assistant Professor of Punjab College of Commerce and Agriculture, Chunni Kalan for research and analytical work to update the book.

Thanks to Mr. Vishal Gupta, Director of GRG Steel Company, Mandi Gobindgarh for motivation and support to complete the book. We are also thankful to dear students Ms Rubina, Ritu , Harinder and Jyoti who participated in editing and contributed in redesigning by incorporating their suggestions. We acknowledge our indebtedness to our families especially, Mr. Inderjit Soni H/O Dr. Anita Soni and Dr. Jaswinder Kumar H/O Dr. Meenu, who gave their valuable assistance and cooperation in bringing this book up in the print. We are also grateful to CA Ajay and Dr. Bhawna, Dr. Nikhil Alluwalia and Master Vivaan Alluwalia for their moral support.

Last but not least, we deeply acknowledge the role of Mr. R.D.S. Bhatia of M/s Regal Publications who has taken personal care in publishing this book.

It is our sincere wish that all students may avail the benefit of this book to brighten their prospects of success in their examination. For any clarification students and teachers are requested to email anitalpu@gmail.com or meenu.rattan@gmail.com.

Dr. Anita Soni
M.Com, MBA (Ex.), Ph.D. UGC NET
Ex member faculty of Economics &
Business Management
GNDU Amritsar.
Member Indian Commerce Association
Principal
Punjab College
Chunni Kalan, Fatehgarh Sahib

Dr. Meenu
M.Com, Ph.D, UGC NET & JRF
Member Indian Commerce Association
Assistant Professor
PG Deptt. of Commerce and Management
DAV College, Sector-10, Chandigarh

SYLLABUS

UNIT - I

Negotiable Instrument Act 1881: Definition of Negotiable Instruments, Features; Promissory Note: Bill of Exchange and Cheque; Holder and Holder in the Due Course; Crossing of a Cheque, Types of Crossing; Negotiation; Dishonour and Discharge of Negotiable Instrument. The Information Technology Act, 2008, Objectives, Regulatory Authorities and Penalties, Cyber Crime-Technical Aspects, Fraud Prevention.

UNIT - II

The Consumer Protection Act 1986: Salient Features, Grievance Redressal Machinery, Environment Protection Act, 1986: Objectives and Scope of the Act, Regulatory Authorities, Environment Pollution-—Offences and Penalties; The Right to Information Act, 2005—Definitions, Right to Information and Obligations of Public Authorities, The Central and State Information Commission, Powers and Functions of the Information Commissions, Appeal and Penalties.

1

NEGOTIABLE INSTRUMENTS

LEARNING OBJECTIVES

1.1 Introduction
1.2 Definition of Negotiable Instrument
1.3 Essential Characteristics of Negotiable Instruments
1.4 Types of Negotiable Instruments
1.5 Conclusion

1.1 INTRODUCTION

Negotiable Instruments have great significance in the modern business world. The chief characteristic of a negotiable instrument is its negotiability, i.e., it can be negotiated from one person to another. It is a transferable document that satisfies certain conditions. These instruments pass freely from hand to hand and thus form an integral part of the modern business mechanism. These instruments have gained prominence as the principal instruments for making payment and discharging business obligations. The Negotiable Instruments Act, 1881 is the legislative enactment of the law relating to three classes of negotiable instruments, namely, Promissory Notes, Bills of Exchange and Cheques which are in common use in monetary transactions.

1.2 DEFINITION OF NEGOTIABLE INSTRUMENT

The term 'negotiable instrument' means a written document which creates a right in favor of some person and which is freely transferable. The Negotiable Instruments Act states that a 'negotiable instrument' means a Promissory Note, Bill of exchange or Cheque payable either to order or to bearer which are transferable from hand to hand by way of negotiation but does not contain words prohibiting transfer or indicating an intention that it shall not be transferable.

Example:

I. Pay to X
II. Pay to X or order
III. Pay to X or bearer/order
IV. Pay to X only
V. An instrument Crossed, "Account payee only"

Since the instrument (d) and (e) are not transferable, i.e. the word only prohibits further transfer and A/C Payee Crossing indicates the intention that it shall not be transferable, these are excluded from negotiable instruments.

Some Important Definitions

According to Justice K.C. Willis: "One the property in which is acquired by any one who takes it bona fide and for value notwithstanding any defect of title in the person from whom he took it."

Possibly the most expressive definition of negotiable instrument has been suggested by **Thomas** as "An instrument is negotiable when it is, by a legally recognized custom of trade or by law, transferable by delivery or by endorsement and delivery, without notice to the party liable, in such a way that—

(a) The holder of it for the time being may sue upon it in his own name, and
(b) The property in it passes to a bona fide transferee for value free from any defect in the title of the person from whom he obtained it."

Examples: Bill of Exchange, Promissory Note, cheques, etc.

1.3 ESSENTIAL CHARACTERISTICS OF NEGOTIABLE INSTRUMENTS

An examination of the above definition reveals the following essential characteristics of negotiable instruments which make them different from an ordinary chattel—

1. **Easy negotiability:** The property in a negotiable instrument is freely transferable. It can be transferable from hand to hand by way of negotiation. In case of order instruments, it is transferable by endorsement and delivery. In case of bearer instruments it is transferable by mere delivery.
2. **Title:** The 'holder in due course' is not in any way affected by the defective title of the transfer of any party. The term holder in due course means a holder who has accepted a negotiable instrument for value, in good faith and before maturity.
3. **Recovery:** The holder in due course is entitled to sue upon the instrument in his own name. Thus, he can recover the amount of the instrument from the party liable for payment on the instrument.
4. **Presumptions:** A negotiable instrument is always subject to certain presumptions. Those will be applicable unless contrary is proved. Example: It is presumed that there is consideration. It is not necessary to write in a promissory note the words "for value received" or similar expressions because the payment of consideration is presumed. The words are usually included to create additional evidence of consideration.
5. **Writing and Signature:** Negotiable Instruments must be written and signed by the parties according to the rules relating to Promissory Notes, Bills of Exchange and Cheques. Demand Drafts are also construel as Negotiable Instruments in the limiting case as they have the same property as N.I. Instruments.
6. **Money:** Negotiable instruments are payable by legal tender money of India. The liabilities of the parties of Negotiable Instruments are fixed and determined in terms of legal tender money.
7. **Notice:** It is not necessary to give notice of transfer of a negotiable instrument to the party liable to pay. The transferee can sue in his own name.

8. **Time for payment**: Negotiable instrument must be payable on demand or at a definite time.
9. **Fixed amount of money:** It must be clear how much money is payable or it must be easily calculable. For example, a note for $1,000 payable at 10% interest in 3 months from x date is sufficient. You actually don't have to have the end result actually calculated in this example. It may also state at the legal rate of interest—where the amount is fixed by statute, it is also negotiable.
10. **Special Procedure**: A special procedure is provided for suits on promissory notes and bills of exchange (The procedure is prescribed in the Civil Procedure Code). A decree can be obtained much more quickly than it can be in ordinary suits.
11. **Popularity**: Negotiable instruments are popular in commercial transactions because of their easy negotiability and quick remedies.
12. **Evidence:** A document which fails to qualify as a negotiable instrument may nevertheless be used as evidence of the fact of indebtedness.

1.4 TYPES OF NEGOTIABLE INSTRUMENTS

Negotiable instruments include two main types: an order to pay (encompasses drafts and cheques) and promises to pay (promissory notes and CDs). The instruments can also be classified as demand instruments or time instruments. Thus, there are four types of negotiable instruments. Examples of negotiable instruments include promissory notes, bills of exchange, cheques and hundi.

Figure 1: Types of Negotiable Instruments

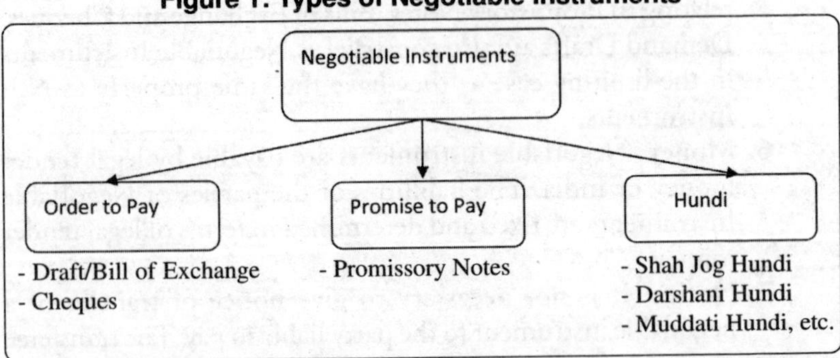

1. (Orders to Pay) Drafts and Cheques

(i) **Draft (or a bill of exchange):** In unconditional written order to pay by which the party creating the draft (the *drawer)* orders another party (the drawee), typically a bank, to pay money to a third party (the *payee)* — e.g., a cheque. (first type of negotiable instrument)—

(a) **Time Draft:** A draft payable at a time certain (definite time)

(b) **Sight Draft:** A draft payable on presentment. It may also be payable on acceptance- where you have the drawee's written promise to pay the draft when it comes due.

(ii) **Cheques:** writer of the cheque is the drawer, the bank on which the cheque is written is the drawee, and the person to whom it is payable is the payee. (second type of negotiable instrument)

2. Promises to Pay (Promissory Note)

Promissory Note: A written promise made by one person (the *maker*) to pay a fixed sum of money to another person (the *payee*) on demand or at a specified *future* time. (third type of negotiable instrument)

3. Hundis

A Hundi is a negotiable instrument by usage. It is often in the form of a bill of exchange drawn in any local language in accordance with the custom of the place. Some times it can also be in the form of a promissory note. A hundi is the oldest known instrument used for the purpose of transfer of money without its actual physical movement. The provisions of the Negotiable Instruments Act shall apply to hundis only when there is no customary rule known to the people.

Types of Hundis

a. **Shah-jog Hundi**: This is drawn by one merchant on another, asking the latter to pay the amount to a Shah. Shah is a respectable and responsible person, a man of worth and known in the bazaar. A shah-jog hundi passes from one hand to another till it reaches a Shah, who, after reasonable enquiries, presents it to the drawee for acceptance of the payment.

b. **Darshani Hundi:** This is a hundi payable at sight. It must be presented for payment within a reasonable time after its receipt by the holder. Thus, it is similar to a demand bill.

c. **Muddati Hundi**: A muddati or miadi hundi is payable after a specified period of time. This is similar to a time bill.

There are few other varieties like Nam-jog hundi, Dhani-jog hundi, Jawabee hundi, Jokhami.

On the basis of nature of negotiable instruments they can be classified as follows:

1. **Demand instrument:** Payable on demand. (demand= instrument states it is payable on sight or demand to a holder), [a holder is the person in possession] A good example of a demand arrangement is a checking account, sometimes called a demand deposit account.
2. **Time instrument:** Payable after a specified time or fixed period of time.
3. **Quasi negotiable instruments**: Quasi negotiable instruments are those which are capable of being transferred by delivery or endorsement but the transferor of the document cannot give a better title to holder that he himself had. **Examples** – Bill of lading, Railway receipt, Dock warrants.

Presumptions as to Negotiable Instruments

Certain presumptions are applicable to all the instruments. According to section 118, until the contrary is proved, the presumptions shall be presumed in all negotiable instruments.

(a) **Consideration**—Every negotiable instrument was made or drawn for consideration, and that every such instrument, when it has been accepted, endorsed, negotiated or transferred, was accepted, endorsed, negotiated or transferred for consideration;

(b) **Date**—Every negotiable instrument bearing a date was made or drawn on such date;

(c) **Time of acceptance**—Every accepted bill of exchange was accepted within a reasonable time after its date and before its maturity;

(d) **Time of transfer**—Every transfer of a negotiable instrument was made before its maturity;

(e) **Order of endorsements**—The endorsements appearing upon a negotiable instrument were made in the order in which they appear thereon;

(f) **Stamps**—A lost promissory note, bill of exchange or cheque was duly stamped;

(g) **That holder is a holder in due course**—The holder of a negotiable instrument is a holder in due course; provided that, where the instrument has been contained from its lawful owner, or from any person in lawful custody thereof, by means of an offence or fraud, or has been obtained from the maker or acceptor thereof by means of an offence or fraud, or for unlawful consideration, the burden of proving that the holder is a holder in due course lies upon him; and

(h) **Presumption on proof of protest.**—In a suit upon an instrument which has been dishonoured, the Court shall, on proof of the protest, presume the fact of dishonour, unless and until such fact is disproved.

1.5 CONCLUSION

1. The term 'negotiable instrument' means a written document which creates a right in favor of some person and which is freely transferable.
2. Essential Characteristics of Negotiable Instruments:
   An examination of the above definition reveals the following essential characteristics of negotiable instruments which make them different from an ordinary chattel—
   1. Easy negotiability
   2. Title
   3. Recovery
   4. Presumptions
   5. Writing and Signature
   6. Money
   7. Notice Time for payment
   8. Fixed amount of money
   9. Special Procedure
   10. Popularity
   11. Evidence
3. Essential elements of the negotiable instruments are:
   1. The Date

2. The Amount
3. Time for Payment
4. Place of payment
5. Stamp

Short Questions

1. Explain Hundi.
2. What is Promissory note?
3. Defined Bills of exchange.
4. Define Cheque.
5. What are various Types of Negotiable Instruments?

Long Questions

1. Explain in details essential characteristics of negotiable instruments.
2. What are various Types of Negotiable Instruments?
3. Explain various Presumptions as to negotiable instruments.
4. Explain various Essential elements of the negotiable instruments.
5. Explain different types of Hundis.

2

PROMISSORY NOTE, BILLS OF EXCHANGE AND CHEQUE

LEARNING OBJECTIVES

2.1 Introduction
2.2 Essential Features of a Promissory Note
2.3 Bill of Exchange
2.4 Essential Features of a Bill of Exchange
2.5 The Procedure for Transfer a Bill of Exchange
2.6 Cheque
2.7 Essential Features of a Cheque
2.8 Difference Between Bill of Exchange and Promissory Note
2.9 Dishonour of Cheques
2.10 Distinguishing Features of Cheques, Bill of Exchange and Promissory Note
2.11 Difference Between a Cheque and a Bill of Exchange
2.12 Other Types of Negotiable Instruments
2.13 Rules Regarding Accommodation Bills

2.1 INTRODUCTION

The **Negotiable Instruments Act** is the Law relating to Promissory Notes, Bills of Exchange and Cheques in India.

The Act applies to the whole of India except the Indian Paper Currency Act, 1871, Section 21, or affects any local usage relating to any instrument in an oriental language. The Act came into force on the first day of March 1882.

The Negotiable Instruments Act deals with three classes of negotiable instruments that are payable either to order or to bearer:

- Promissory Notes
- Bills of Exchanges
- Cheques

Promissory Note

Simply stated, a promissory note is a promise to pay or 'I Owe You'. It is a formal commitment between two parties that is usually necessary when money is borrowed and lent between them. All business loans secured from a bank or other lending institutions have some sort of promissory note, but they are also recommended for loans between two individuals to avoid any misunderstandings or possible legal troubles. Promissory note is a signed document containing a written promise to pay a stated sum to a specified person or the bearer at a specified date or on demand. It involves to parties the maker and the payee.

According to Negotiable Instruments Act, 1881, Section 4

> "A promissory note is an instrument in writing (not being a bank note or a currency note) containing an unconditional undertaking, signed by the maker, to pay a certain sum of money only or to the order of a certain person, or to the bearer of the instrument."

Thus, a *promissory note* is a legal instrument (more particularly, a financial instrument), in which one party (the maker or issuer) promises in writing to pay a determinate sum of money to the other (the payee), either at a fixed or determinable future time or on demand of the payee, under specific terms.

A promissory note is drawn and signed by the debtor, who promises to pay the creditor a certain sum of money. The specimen of promissory note is given below:

> Dhaka 11003
> Tk 8,000 5th April, 2007
>
> Three months after date I promise to pay Mr. Harun the sum of Takas eight thousand, for value received.
>
> Stamp
> To Mr. Harun Sd. Hasanur Rahman

A promissory note may be drawn by more than one person also who may undertake to pay the amount both in their individual capacities as well as jointly. The specimen of a promissory note with joint and several liabilities is given below:

> Tk …………
> Dhaka……………..20………
>
> On demand we jointly and severally promise to pay to………………………………………
> ………………………………………………………………………………………………
> ……………………………………………………………....or order the sum of Takas
> ……………………………………………………………………............ together with
> interest on such sum from this date at the rate of ……………………………………
> percent per annum with …………………………... rests, for value received.
>
> Stamp
> (Signature across the stamp)
> Addresses……………..

2.2 ESSENTIAL FEATURES OF A PROMISSORY NOTE

The essential characteristics of a promissory note may be summarized as follows:

1. It must be in writing
2. It must certain a promise or undertaking to pay
3. The promise to pay must be unconditional
4. It must be signed by the maker
5. The maker must be a certain person
6. The payee must be certain
7. The sum payable must be certain
8. The amount payable must be in legal tender money
9. Other formalities

2.3 BILL OF EXCHANGE

According to Negotiable Instruments Act, 1881, Section 5,

> "A bill of exchange is an instrument in writing containing an unconditional order, signed by the maker, directing a certain person to pay a certain sum of money only to, or to the order of, a certain person or to the bearer of the instrument."

That is, a bill of exchange contains an order from the creditor to the debtor to pay a specified amount to a person mentioned therein. The maker of a bill is called the 'drawer', the person who is directed to pay is called the 'drawee'; the person who is entitled to receive the payment is called the 'payee'; sometimes the drawer himself is the payee. The specimen of a bill of exchange is given below:

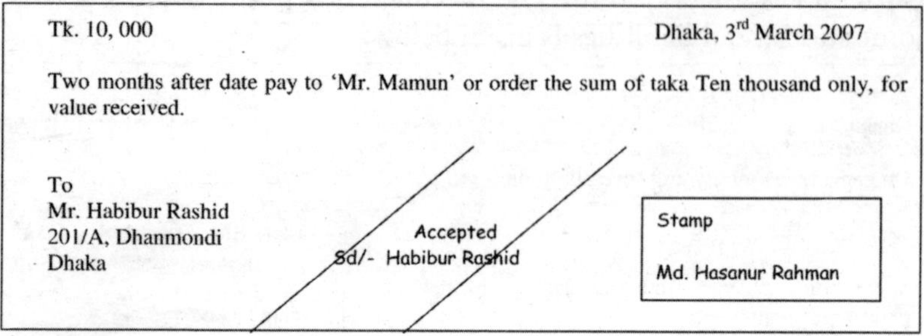

Tk. 10, 000 Dhaka, 3rd March 2007

Two months after date pay to 'Mr. Mamun' or order the sum of taka Ten thousand only, for value received.

To
Mr. Habibur Rashid
201/A, Dhanmondi
Dhaka

Accepted
Sd/- Habibur Rashid

Stamp

Md. Hasanur Rahman

2.4 ESSENTIAL FEATURES OF A BILL OF EXCHANGE

The essential characteristics of a bill of exchange may be summarized as follows:

1. It must be in writing
2. It must contain an order to pay
3. The order to pay must be unconditional
4. It must be signed by drawer
5. The drawer, drawee and payee must be certain
6. The sum payable must be certain
7. The bill must contain an order to pay money only
8. It must comply with the formalities as regards date, consideration, stamps, etc.

2.5 THE PROCEDURE FOR TRANSFER A BILL OF EXCHANGE

A bill of exchange is negotiated when it transferred from one person to another person. So it constitutes a transferee of the holder of the bill. A valid transferred always depends on the classes of the bill. If the bill is payable to the bearer there is a valid negotiation by means of delivery. The person who posses the bill and therefore the holder of the bill is entitled to sue on the bill in his own name. A bill is said to an order bill if it validly negotiates. The following condition must be fulfil—

(1) There has been a endorsement by the prior holder. The name of the new possessor is specified on the reserves of the bill.
(2) A conditional and partial endorsement shall be null and void.
(3) The bill has been delivered to the possessor and physical possession must be given to the transferee.

Prerequisites for Enforcement

If a bill is properly presented and refuses to acceptance the bill has been dishonored by non-acceptance or non-payment then an immediate right to recourse arises against the other parties to the bill. The right to recourse is lost if the prerequisites for the enforcement are not properly fulfilled.

1. **Presentment of payment**—A bill must be presented to the drawee or his authorized agent on the due date at the proper place. Presentation of bill is unnecessary where it has already been dishonored by non-acceptance.
2. **Notice of dishonor**—A notice of dishonor must be given to the drawer and to the endorser, to preserve their liability within a reasonable time.
3. **Protest**—After the notice of dishonor additional step should be taken in case of foreign bill. The bill must be protest by the holder. Protest means obtaining a legal proof of dishonor.

Remedies of Dishonour

When a bill of exchange is dishonored by non-acceptance or non-payment the holder can sue against all the parties liable for the bill. Notice of dishonor must be given to the concerning parties before filling the suit. The notice shall contain the fact of dishonored, the date of dishonor, the reason of dishonor. When the bill is dishonor the holder passes the bill to a notary public who again presents the bill for payment, if dishonor then the notary public will drawn up an official certificate for evidencing such dishonor.

1. If the drawee refuses to accept the bill when it is presented before him for acceptance, it is called dishonor by non-acceptance.
2. If the drawer has accepted the bill, but on the due date, he refuses to make payment of the bill, it is called dishonor by non-payment

2.6 CHEQUE

According to the Negotiable Instruments Act, 1881, Section 6,

" A cheque is a bill of exchange drawn on a specified banker and not expressed to be payable otherwise than on demand."

It is an important document for any transaction in the business world. Thus, a cheque is a bill of exchange with two distinctive features, namely—

(1) It is always drawn on a bank
(2) It is always payable on demand

2.7 ESSENTIAL FEATURES OF A CHEQUE

(1) A cheque is printed paper
(2) On the printed paper it specifies the bank and branch address
(3) It must be in writing
(4) A cheque is always drawn on a banker
(5) A cheque can only be drawn payable on demand
(6) It must have a date
(7) Cheque No. is also exist
(8) It must contain an order to pay
(9) It includes an account No. of owner of the account holder
(10) The order to pay must be unconditional
(11) The sun payable must be certain
(12) A cheque must contain an order to pay money only

Specimen of a Cheque

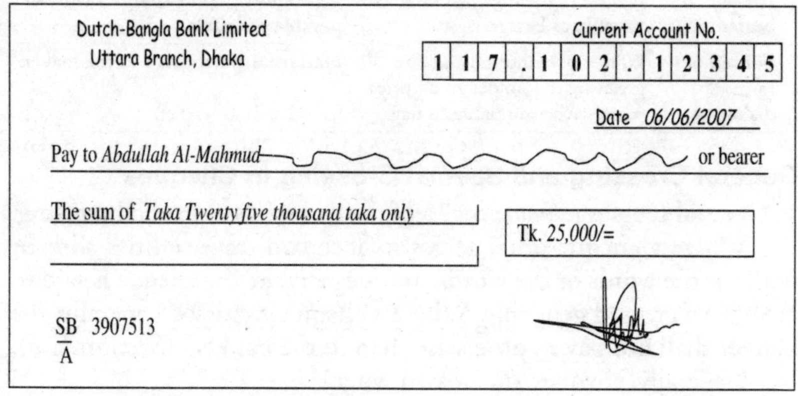
Dutch-Bangla Bank Limited
Uttara Branch, Dhaka
Current Account No.
1 1 7 . 1 0 2 . 1 2 3 4 5
Date 06/06/2007
Pay to Abdullah Al-Mahmud or bearer
The sum of Taka Twenty five thousand taka only
Tk. 25,000/=
SB 3907513
A

2.8 DIFFERENCE BETWEEN BILL OF EXCHANGE AND PROMISSORY NOTE

Particulars	*Bill of Exchange*	*Promissory note*
1. Definition	A bill of exchange is an instrument in writing containing an unconditional order, signed by the maker, directing a certain person to pay a certain sum of money only to, or to the order of, a certain person or to the bearer of the instrument.	A promissory note is an instrument in writing (not being a bank note or a currency note) containing an unconditional undertaking, signed by the maker, to pay a certain sum of money only or to the order of a certain person, or to the bearer of the instrument.
2. Number of parties	In a bill of exchange there are three parties—the drawer, drawee and payee.	In a promissory note there are two parties—the maker of the note and the payee.
3. Promise and order	A bill of exchange is an order for making the payment.	A promissory note contains a promise to make the payment.
4. Acceptance	Bill payable after sight requires acceptance of the drawee before it is presented for payment.	Promissory note does not require it.
5. Nature of liability	The liability of drawer of a bill of exchange is secondary and conditional.	The liability of the maker of a promissory note is primary and absolute.
6. Maker's position	The maker or drawer of an accepted bill stands in immediate relation with the acceptor and not the payee.	The maker of promissory note stands in immediate relation with the payee.

Particulars	*Bill of Exchange*	*Promissory note*
7. Payable to bearer	A bill of exchange can be drawn payable to bearer.	A promissory note cannot be drawn payable to bearer.
8. Formalities in case of dishonor	Notice of dishonor must be given by the holder to all prior parties who are liable to pay.	No notice is necessary to the maker.

General Crossing and Special Crossing in Cheques

1. General crossing: Section 123 of the Act refers to general crossing.

Where a cheque bears across its face two traverse lines with or without the words or the words "not negotiable, the cheque is said to have been crossed generally. Where a cheque is crossed generally, the banker shall not pay it, otherwise than to the banker" (Section 126).

Generally, cheques are crossed when—

1. There are two transverse parallel lines, marked across its face or
2. The cheque bears an abbreviation "**& Co.**" between the two parallel lines, or
3. The cheque bears the words "**Not Negotiable**" between the two parallel lines, or
4. The cheque bears the words "**A/c. Payee**" between the two parallel lines.

A crossed cheque can be made **bearer cheque** by cancelling the crossing and writing that the crossing is cancelled and affixing the full signature of drawer.

Specimen of General Crossing!

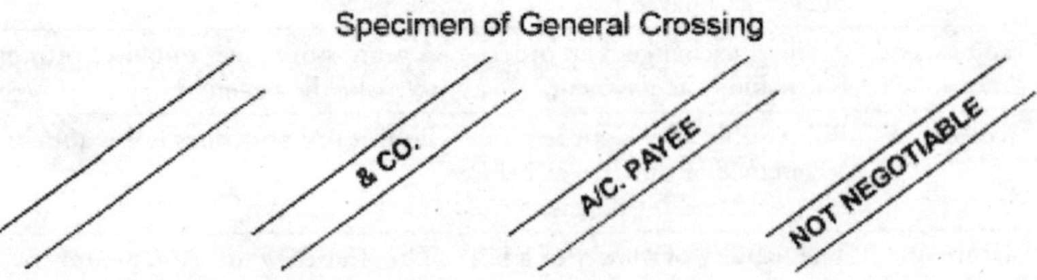

2. Special crossing: Section 124 of the Act refers to Special crossing.

Where a cheque bears across its face in addition to the name of the banker either with or without the words or the words 'not negotiable, then the cheque is said to have been crossed specially. The object of special crossing is to direct the banker to pay the cheque only if it is presented through the particular bank mentioned.

When a particular bank's name is written in between the two parallel lines the cheque is said to be specially crossed.

Specimen of Special or Restrictive Crossing!

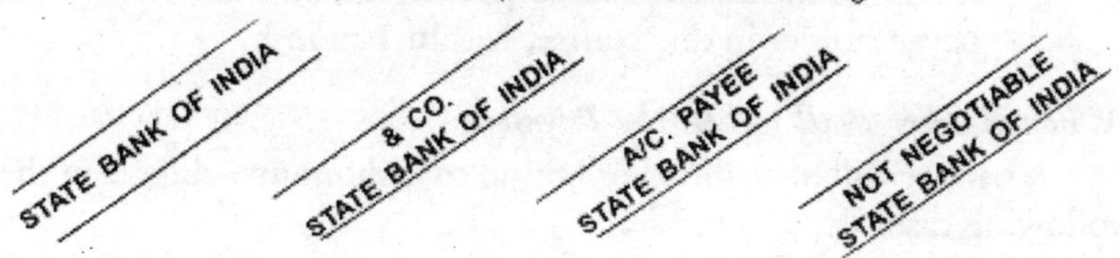

In addition to the word bank, the words "**A/c. Payee Only**", "**Not Negotiable**" may also be written. The payment of such cheque is not made unless the bank named in crossing is presenting the cheque. The effect of special crossing is that the bank makes payment only to the banker whose name is written in the crossing. Specially crossed cheques are more safe than a generally crossed cheques.

2.9 DISHONOUR OF CHEQUES

Section 92 of the Negotiable Instruments Act states that –

"A promissory note, bill of exchange or cheque is said to be dishonored by non-payment when the maker of the note and acceptor of the bill makes default in payment."

Dishonour of Cheque is an Offence

Section 138 of the Negotiable Instruments Act states that, A banker shall return the cheque when the money standing to the credit of the account holder is insufficient to honour the cheque.

Dishonour of cheque is a criminal offence. The drawer shall be deemed to have committed an offence and such offence will be punishable with imprisonment and with fine (*imprisonment shall be extend 1 years or fine twice the amount of the cheque or both*).

Provisions of Section 138 of the Act are Applicable only if –

(a) The cheque is issued for discharge of a liability only. A cheque given as gift will not fall in this category.
(b) The cheque is presented to the bank for payment within 6 months or its specific validity period, whichever is earlier.

(c) The payee or holder in due course has given notice demanding payment within **30** days of the receiving information of dishonour as regarding the insufficiency of funds.
(d) The drawer does not make payment within **30** days of the receipt of the notice. The complaint can be made only by the payee/holder in due course, within **1** month.

When Banker shall Refuse the Payment

A banker will be justified or bound to dishonour a cheque in the following cases if—

(1) The cheque is undated.
(2) The cheque is stale, i.e. it has not been presented within the validity period of the cheque.
(3) The instrument is inchoate (unclear or unformed or tentative) or not free from reasonable doubt.
(4) The cheque is post-dated and presented for payment before its ostensible date.
(5) Authority of the banker to honour a cheque of his customer is determined by the notice of the drawer's death, lunacy and insolvency. However, any payment made prior to the receipt of the notice of death is valid.
(6) Bank receives notice in respect of closure of the account.
(7) The cheque contains material alterations, irregular signature of irregular endorsement.
(8) The customer has countermanded payment.
(9) Any difference between the amount of cheque in words and in figures.
(10) Any irregular endorsements.
(11) The cheque is mutilated.
(12) Signature of the drawer has been forged.

2.10 DISTINGUISHING FEATURES OF CHEQUES, BILL OF EXCHANGE AND PROMISSORY NOTE

1. Instruments in writing: The law requires that a cheque, bill or promissory note must be an instrument in writing. It does not specify any particular material with which it is to be written. Though a negotiable instruments written with a pencil is not prohibited by law, in practice the bankers do not accept such instruments because of risk involved. Alternations therein may be easily made which cannot be detected.

2. Unconditional order/promise: A cheque and a bill of exchange contain an order to the drawee whereas a promissory note contains a promise by the maker to his creditor. The promise in the former and the order in the latter must be an unconditional one i.e., the payment should not be made dependent upon the happening or occurrence of a particular event or on the fulfilment of any condition. But if the time for payment of the amount (or any of its instalments) is expressed to be on the lapse of a certain period after the occurrence of specified event, the promise or order to pay is not deemed 'conditional' provided the event is certain to happen according to ordinary expectation of mankind, although the time of its happening may be uncertain (Section 5). The words in the cheque or the bill must be in the nature of an order rather than a request, though it is not necessary that the word 'order' is specifically mentioned therein. The words in the promissory note should also amount to an unconditional promise to pay the specified amount, otherwise it will not be treated as a promissory note. For example, in the following cases, unconditional promise is not given by the writer of the note:

- Mr. B.I.O.U. (I owe you) Rs. 500.
- I am liable to pay you Rs. 500.
- "I promise to pay B Rs. 500 and all other sums which shall be due to him".
- "I promise to pay B Rs. 500, first deducting there out any money which he may owe me".
- "I promise to pay B Rs. 500 seven days after my marriage with C".
- "I promise to pay B Rs. 500 on D's death, provided D leaves me enough to pay that sum".
- "I promise to pay B Rs. 500 and to deliver him my black horse on 1st January next".
- (i) I promise to pay B or order Rs. 5000.
  (ii) I acknowledge myself indebted to B in Rs. 1000 to be paid on demand, for value received.

3. The drawee of a cheque or bill: A cheque is always drawn on and is payable by a banker specified therein, while a bill of exchange may be drawn on any person, firm or company. Thus, only a customer of a bank having a current or a savings bank account is entitled to draw a cheque on his banker i.e., the particular branch of a bank where he has opened his bank account. The name and address of the drawee bank are specifically printed on the cheque form. A bill of exchange is generally drawn by a seller on his customer, or by a creditor on his debtor. Sometimes accommodation bills are also drawn to help a familiar party.

4. The amount of the instrument must be certain: The order of the drawer of a cheque or a bill and the promise by the writer of a promissory note must be to pay a certain sum of money and not anything else, e.g., securities or goods, etc. The amount of money to be paid must be certain and specified in words and figures.

5. The instrument must be payable either 'to order' or 'to bearer': According to Section 13, a promissory note, bill of exchange or cheque must be payable either 'to order' or 'to bearer'.

(i) **Payable to order:** A promissory note, bill of exchange or cheque is payable to order if it is expressed to be so payable For example, if a cheque is drawn as "Pay to Ram Lal" its payment may be made to Ram Lal or any person as per his order. The cheque can be endorsed, even if it does not contain the words "or order". But if the cheque is drawn as "Pay to Ram Lal only", it cannot be endorsed by Ram Lal because the word "only" shows the intention of the drawer to restrict its further transfer. Such a cheque shall be payable to Ram Lal only.

If a negotiable instrument, either originally or by endorsement, is expressed to be payable to the order of a specified person, and not to him or his order, it is nevertheless payable to him or his order at his option. For example, if a bill of exchange is expressed as 'pay to the order of Radhey Shyam or order", it is still payable to Radhey Shyam or if he so chooses to the person specified by him.

(ii) **Payable to bearer:** A promissory note, bill of exchange and cheque are payable to bearer (a) if it is expressed to be so payable, or (b) if the only or the last endorsement is an endorsement in blank. This means a cheque payable 'to order' becomes a bearer cheque if it is endorsed in blank.

6. The payee must be a certain person: The person to whom payment of the instrument is to be made must be certain. The payee is considered as 'certain person' for this purpose even if he is mis-named or is designated by description only (Section 5). The term 'person' includes, besides individuals, bodies corporate, local authorities societies and associations of persons, etc., and cheque may be drawn payable to the Registrar, Principal, Director, Secretary, etc., of these institutions.

7. The payee may be more than one person: A negotiable instrument may be made payable to two or more payees jointly or it may be made payable in the alternative to one of two or one of some of several payees [Section 13(2)]. For example, a cheque may be payable to Ram and Shyam or Ram or Shyam. In both these cases, it is payable to a certain person.

8. The time of payment: A cheque is always payable on demand, through words to this effect are not mentioned therein. A bill may be payable at sight or after a period of time specified therein. A promissory note or a bill of exchange in which no time for payment is specified is payable on demand (Section 19). If a bill is payable after a certain period it must be accepted by a drawee.

9. Signature of the drawer/promissor: A negotiable instrument is valid only if it bears the signature of the drawer/promisor. In case of a cheque the signature of the drawer must tally with his specimen signature given to the banker at the time of opening his account.

10. Delivery of a instrument is essential: A promissory note, bill of exchange and the cheque is a negotiable instrument. The making, acceptance or endorsement of such an instrument is completed by delivery (Section 46). This means that a negotiable instrument is deemed to have been drawn, when it is written by the person concerned and delivered to the other party to whom it is meant. Delivery may be either actual or constructive.

11. Stamping of promissory notes and bills of exchange is necessary: The Indian Stamp Act, 1899 requires that the promissory note and the bills of exchange must be stamped. This is not required in case of a cheque. The value of stamp depends upon the value of the note or the bill and whether it is payable on demand or at a future date. A note or bill without stamp cannot be admitted in evidence. It may be stamped either before or at the time of its execution.

2.11 DIFFERENCE BETWEEN A CHEQUE AND A BILL OF EXCHANGE

Cheque differs from a bill of exchange in the following respects:

1. Drawee

A cheque is always drawn on a bank or a banker while a bill of exchange can be drawn on any person including a banker.

2. Acceptance

A cheque does not require any acceptance while a bill must be accepted before the drawee can be made liable upon it.

3. Payment

A cheque is payable immediately on demand without any days of grace, but a bill of exchange is normally entitled to three days of grace unless it is payable on demand. The drawer of a bill is discharged from liability, if it is not duly presented for payment, but the drawer of a cheque will not be discharged by delay of the holder in presenting it for payment, unless through the delay, the drawer has been injured, e.g., by the failure of the bank the drawer has lost the money which would have otherwise discharged the amount of the cheque. However, where the drawer is so discharged, the payee may rank as creditor of the bank for the amount of the cheque

4. Crossing

A cheque may be crossed but there is no such provision in the case of a bill of exchange.

5. Notice of Dishonor

When a cheque is not met, notice of dishonor is not necessary. Want of assets in the hands of the banker is sufficient notice. It is necessary to give a notice of dishonor in order to make the drawer of a bill liable.

6. Payable to Bearer on Demand

A cheque can be drawn payable to bearer on demand. But a bill of exchange cannot be so drawn.

7. Stamp

A bill of exchange must be stamped, whereas a cheque does not require any stamp.

8. Countermanding Payment

A cheque may be revoked by countermand of payment. The payment of a bill, however, cannot be countermanded.

9. Noting and Protesting

A cheque is not noted or protested for dishonor and is generally inland.

10. Presentment

A bill of exchange must be duly presented for payment otherwise the drawer will be discharged. The drawer of a cheque is not discharged by failure of the holder to present it in due time unless the drawer has sustained damage by the delay.

11. Protection

A banker is given statutory protection with regard to payment of cheques in certain circumstances. No such protection is available to the drawee or acceptor of a bill of exchange.

12. Validity

A 'payable to bearer on demand' is valid but a bill drawn 'payable to bearer on demand' is absolutely void and illegal (though cheque drawn a bill can be made payable to the bearer after a certain time) (Sec. 31, The Reserve Bank of India Act).

13. Grace Period

Three days of grace are allowed while calculating the maturity date in the case of 'time bills' (i.e., bills drawn payable after the expiry of a certain period). Since a cheque is always payable on demand, there is no question of allowing any days of grace.

14. Parties

There are three parties to a bill of exchange, namely, the drawer, the drawee and the payee, while in a promissory note there are only two parties—maker and payee.

15. Liability

The liability of a maker of a bill of exchange is primary and while the liability of a drawer of a bill of exchange is secondary and conditional. It arises only when the drawee fails to pay that the drawer would be liable as a surety.

2.12 OTHER TYPES OF NEGOTIABLE INSTRUMENTS

1. **Inland instrument.**—A promissory note, bill of exchange or cheque drawn or made in [India] and made payable in, or drawn upon any person resident in [Indian] shall be deemed to be an inland instrument.
2. **Section 12: Foreign instrument**—Any such instrument not so drawn, made or made payable shall be deemed to be a foreign instrument.
3. **Section 17: Ambiguous instruments**—Where an instrument may be construed either as a promissory note or bill of exchange, the holder may at his election treat it as either and the instrument shall be thenceforward treated accordingly.
4. **Section 19: Instruments payable on demand**—A promissory note or bill of exchange, in which no time for payment is specified, and, a cheque, are payable on demand.
5. **Section 20: Inchoate stamped instruments.**—Where one person signs and delivers to another a paper stamped in accordance with the law relating to negotiable instruments then in force in India, and either wholly blank or having written thereon an incomplete negotiable instrument, he thereby gives *prima facie* authority to the holder thereof to make or complete, as then case may be, upon it a negotiable instrument, instrument, for any amount specified therein and not exceeding the amount covered by the stamp. The person so signing shall be liable upon such instrument, in the capacity in which he signed the same, to any holder in due course for such amount, provided that no person other than a holder in due course shall recover from the person delivering the instrument anything in excess of the amount intended by him to be paid thereunder.
6. **Section 21: At sight, On presentment, After sight**—In a promissory note or bill of exchange the expressions "at sight" and "on presentment" means on demand. The expression "after sight" means, in a promissory note, after presentment for sight, and, in a bill of exchange after acceptance, or noting for non-acceptance, or nothing for non-acceptance, or protest for non-acceptance.
7. **Order Instrument**—An order instrument is a negotiable instrument that is payable to the order of an identified person or to

an identifiable person or order. The person must be named with certainty (except in a bearer instrument). Any instrument payable to the following is a bearer instrument.

8. Bearer Instrument—A negotiable instrument payable to bearer or to cash, rather than to an identifiable payee. Bearer: The person possessing a bearer instrument.

(i) Payable to the order of bearer;
(ii) Payable to Jane Smith or bearer;
(iii) Payable to bearer;
(iv) Pay cash; or
(v) Pay to the order of cash.

Accomodation Bill (Exception I to Sec. 43)

Many bills are drawn and accepted without any consideration; the various parties sign the bills for the purpose of lending their names to oblige their friends. Such bills are called accommodation bills. An accommodation bill is one for which no consideration has been given by the drawer to the acceptor for the purpose of accommodating some other party who is to use it and is expected to pay it when due. The party accommodating is called the "accommodation party". The party accommodated is called the "accommodated party". When a person endorses a bill without consideration, he is called a "backer" and the operation is called "backing the bill." **Example:** P is in need of Rs. 2000. He approaches Q for this purpose. Q agrees to help him and proposes P to draw a bill on him. Which he would accept. P can get the bill discounted with his banker? On or before the due date P will have to provide Q with the necessary funds to enable him to meet his acceptance. Thus, P is in a position to raise money for the term of the bill. Such a bill which has been drawn and accepted without consideration is called an accommodation bill.

2.13 RULES REGARDING ACCOMMODATION BILLS

1. The accommodation party is liable on the bill to a holder for value. Thus, in the above example, if P endorses the bill to C, his creditor, C can recover the amount of the bill from Q.
2. An accommodation bill may be negotiated after maturity and the holder of such a bill can recover thereon, provided he takes it in good faith and for value. (Sec. 59).
3. The drawer is not discharged on account of the non-

presentment of accommodation bill to the acceptor (Sec. 76).
4. In the case of an accommodation bill, the failure to give notice of dishonor will not discharge the prior parties from liability (Sec. 98).

Fictitious bill.—A bill in which the drawer or the payee or both are non existent. In such case the drawee or the acceptor is liable to pay the due amount to the holder in due course. The onus to prove that the drawer is fake lies on the endorsee. He can prove it by proving that the signature of drawer and first endorser are the same.

Documentery bill.—In international trading, a bill of exchange or commercial draft that is presented for payment with the required documents such as a clean bill of lading, certificate of insurance, certificate of origin. Also called documentary draft.

Undated bills.—Where the date of a bill is not mentioned and where the date of the acceptance of a bill, payable at a fixed period after sight is omitted, any holder may insert the true date of issue or acceptance as the case may be and such insertion is not considered to be a material alteration. The instrument will not be considered to be invalid merely because it is undated.

Banker's draft. It is an order addressed by one bank to another or by a bank to its branch directing the latter to pay a specified sum of money to a named person or his order. These drafts are drawn either against cash deposited at the time of their purchase or against debits to current accounts with the bankers. A bank draft is similar to a cheque in some respects but there are certain points of distinction between the two.

2.14 CONCLUSION

1. Promissory note is a signed document containing a written promise to pay a stated sum to a specified person or the bearer at a specified date or on demand. It involves two parties—the maker of the note and the payee.
2. A cheque is a bill of exchange drawn on a specified banker and not expressed to be payable otherwise than on demand.
3. A bill of exchange contains an order from the creditor to the debtor to pay a specified amount to a person mentioned therein. The

maker of a bill is called the 'drawer', the person who is directed to pay is called the 'drawee'; the person who is entitled to receive the payment is called the 'payee'.

4. **Features of Bill/Promissory Note and a Cheque**
    1. Instruments in writing.
    2. Unconditional order/promise.
    3. The drawee of a cheque or bill.
    4. The amount of the instrument must be certain.
    5. The instrument must be payable either 'to order' or 'to bearer'.
    6. The payee must be a certain person.
    7. The payee may be more than one person.
    8. The time of payment.
    9. Signature of the drawer/promissor.
    10. Delivery of a instrument is essential.
    11. Stamping of promissory notes and bills of exchange is necessary.

SHORT QUESTIONS

1. What is promissory note?
2. Define BILL of exchange.
3. What are the Essential features of a bill of exchange?
4. What is procedure for transfer a bill of exchange?
5. Define Cheque.
6. What is the difference between bill of exchange and Promissory Note?
7. What are the Essential features of a Cheque?
8. General Crossing and Special Crossing in cheques.
9. Write short note on Dishonour of cheques.
10. Distinguish the features of Cheques, bill of exchange and Promissory Note.

LONG QUESTIONS

1. What is promissory note? What are the Essential features of promissory notes?
2. Define BILL of exchange. What are the Essential features of a Bill of Exchange?
3. What is procedure for transfer a bill of exchange?
4. What is the difference between bill of exchange and Promissory Note?

5. What are the Essential features of a Cheque? What is the difference between General Crossing and Special Crossing in cheques?
6. Distinguish the features of Cheques, bill of exchange and Promissory Note.
7. Why are bill of exchange, Promissory Notes and Cheques called negotiable indtruments?

PRACTICAL PROBLEMS

Attempt the following problems, giving reasons:

1. Are the following instruments promissory notes:
   (a) "I promise to pay B Rs. 5,000 on the death of C provided he leaves me sufficient amount to pay the sum." (Signed by A)
   (b) "Received from B the sum of one thousand rupees to be paid after three months with interest at 15 per cent per annum. Dated may 19, 2007." (Signed by A)
   (c) "I acknowledge myself to be indebted to B in Rs. 5,000 to be paid on demand to B on his attaining the age of majority". (Signed by A)

   [*Hint:* (a) No. (b) No. (c) No. (Sec. 4))]
2. A bill is drawn, payable at 50, Lucknow Road, Kanpur but does not contain the name of the drawee. B who resides at 50, Lucknow Road, Kanpur accepts the bill. Is it a valid bill?
   [*Hint:* Yes, When B accepts it, he holds out by his acceptance that he is the person to whom the bill is directed [Sec. 54; *Gray v. Milner*. (1810) 8 Taunt 739.]
3. A bill is drawn "Pay to A or order the sum of one thousand rupees." In the margin the amount stated is Rs 10,000 in figures. (a) Is this a valid bill? (b) If so, for what amount?
   [*Hint:* (a) Yes. (b) Rs. 1,000 (Sec.18).]
4. A signs as maker a blank stamped paper and gives it to B, and authorizes him to fill it as a note for Rs. 500, to secure an advance which C is to make to B. B fraudulently fills it up as a note for Rs. 2,000, payable to C who has in good faith advanced Rs. 2,000. Can C recover Rs. 2,000?
   [*Hint:* Yes (Sec. 20).]
5. A signs, as acceptor, a bill bearing an 80 P. stamp with the amount left blank. The amount of Rs 100 in the margin is fraudulently

altered to Rs. 1,000, and the bill is, in words, filled in for a thousand rupees. The bill gets into the hands of H, a holder in due course. Can he recover this amount?
[*Hint:* Yes, (*Lloyds Bank Ltd v. Cooke*, (1907) 1 K.B. 795; Sec. 20).]

6. A bill of exchange is payable to Shyam or order. At maturity another person of the same name wrongfully gets possession of the bill and presents it to the acceptor for payment. After being satisfied that the person presenting is Shyam, the acceptor makes payment on it in due course. Is the acceptor discharged?
[*Hint:* No, (Sec. 100)]

7. D drew a bill on A in favour of P. The bill was payable on demand. When the payee sought to present the bill for acceptance or payment, he discovered that no such person as A existed. (a) Is this valid bill? (b) To whom should P go for the money?
[*Hint:* (a) No, as the drawee is not certain (Sec. 5) (b) D]

8. W dismissed his servant R from service and for his wages gave him a draft in the following words: "Mr. N will much oblige Mr. W by paying to Mr. R or order, rupees two hundred on his account. Signed by W." Is this draft a bill of exchange?
[*Hint:* Yes, as the introduction of the words of gratitude does not destroy the order to pay [*Ruff v. Webb*, (1794) 5 R.R. 733)]

9. A company issued a cheque on its banker. A receipt was appended to the cheque and it ordered the banker to make the payment "provided the receipt form at foot hereof is duly signed, stamped and dated." Is the cheque valid?
[*Hint:* No, because its payment is made conditional upon signing of the receipt (*Bevin v. London & South Western Bank Ltd.* (1890) 1 K.B. 270).]

10. A accepts a bill for the accommodation of B (the drawer). The bill is dishonoured by A on the due date and C, the holder of the bill, on that date, collects the amount from B. (a) Can B sue A for the recovery of the amount? (b) Will it make any difference, if the bill gets into the hands of a holder in due course and he files a suit against A for the recovery of the amount?
[*Hint:* (a) No, B cannot sue A for the recovery of the amount on the bill (Exception 1 to Sec. 43). (b) The holder in due course can recover the amount from A.]

3

Parties to Negotiable Instruments

LEARNING OBJECTIVES

3.1 Parties to Negotiable Instruments
3.2 Liability of Parties
3.3 Holder and Holder in Due Course
3.4 Privileges of Holder in Due Course
3.5 Difference between Holder and Holder in Due Course
3.6 Holder for Value
3.7 Payment in Due Course
3.8 Conclusion

3.1 PARTIES TO NEGOTIABLE INSTRUMENTS

3.1.1 Parties to a Bill of Exchange

Following are the parties to a Bill of Exchange:

1. **The Drawer:** The person who draws a bill of exchange is called the drawer.
2. **The Drawee:** The party on whom such bill of exchange is drawn and who is directed to pay is called the drawee.

3. **The Acceptor**: The person who accepts the bill is known as the acceptor. Normally the drawee is the acceptor. But a stranger can also accept a bill on behalf of the drawee.
4. **The Payee:** The person to whom the amount of the bill is payable is called the payee.
5. **The Endorser**: When the holder transfers or endorses the instrument to any other person the holder becomes the Endorser.
6. **The Endorsee:** The person to whom the bill is endorsed is called the endorsee.
7. **The Holder**: Holder of bill of exchange means any person who is legally entitled to the possession of it and to receive or recover the amount due thereon form the parties. He is either the payee or the endorsee. The finder of a lost bill payable to bearer or a person in wrongful possession of such instrument is not a holder.
8. **Drawee in case of need**: The drawer of a bill or even an endorser may write in the instrument the name of a person directing the holder to resort to such person in case of need. Such a person is called a drawee in case of need. He is merely in the position of a drawee who has not accepted the bill. The bill cannot be presented to him for acceptance but only for payment.

   Where a drawee in case of need is mentioned in the bill such a bill is not dishonored until it has been dishonored by such a drawee in case of need. The effect of this provision is to make the presentment to the drawee in case of need obligatory on the part of the holder.
9. **Acceptor for Honour**: Any person may voluntarily become a party to a bill as an acceptor by accepting it for the honour of the drawer or of any person. When the original drawee refuses to accept or refuses to furnish better security when demanded by a notary, any person may step in to safeguard the honor of the drawer or any endorser and bind himself by an acceptance. The effect of such acceptance is that the bill is treated as alive and is not considered to be dishonored till it is dishonored by the acceptor for honor.

3.1.2 Parties to a Promissory Note

Following are the parties to a Promissory Note—

1. **The Maker:** He is the person who promises to pay the amount stated in the promissory note.

2. **The Payee**: The person named in the promissory note to whom the money is payable.
3. **The Holder:** He may be either the payee or someone else to whom the promissory note has been endorsed.
4. **The Endorser**: When the holder transfers or endorses the instrument to any other person the holder becomes the Endorser.
5. **The Endorsee**: The person to whom the bill is endorsed is called the endorsee.

3.1.3 Parties to a Cheque: Following are the Parties to a Cheque

1. **The Drawee:** He is the person who draws the cheque.
2. **The Drawee:** The banker on whom the cheque is drawn.
3. **The Payee:** The person to whom the amount of the bill is payable is called the payee.
4. **The Holder**: Holder of bill of exchange means any person who is legally entitled to the possession of it and to receive or recover the amount due thereon form the parties. He is either the payee or the endorsee. The finder of a lost bill payable to bearer or a person in wrongful possession of such instrument is not a holder.
5. **The Endorser**: When the holder transfers or endorses the instrument to any other person the holder becomes the Endorser.
6. **The Endorsee:** The person to whom the bill is endorsed is called the endorsee.

3.2 LIABILITY OF PARTIES

Article V of the Negotiable Instrument Act deals with the liability of parties.

Section 60. The maker of a negotiable instrument by making it engages that he will pay it according to its tenor, and admits the existence of the payee and his then capacity to indorse.

Section 61. The drawer by drawing the instrument admits the existence of the payee and his then capacity to indorse, and engages that on due presentment the instrument will be accepted or paid, or both, according to its tenor, and that if it be dishonored, and the necessary proceedings on dishonor be duly taken, he will pay the amount thereof to the holder, or to any indorser who may be compelled to pay it. But the drawer may insert in the instrument an express stipulation negativing or limiting his own liability to the holder.

Section 62. The acceptor by accepting the instrument engages that he will pay it according to the tenor of his acceptance and admits:

1. The existence of the drawer, the genuineness of his signature, and his capacity and authority to draw the instrument; and
2. The existence of the payee and his then capacity to indorse.

Section 63. A person placing his signature upon an instrument otherwise than as maker, drawer or acceptor is deemed to be an indorser, unless he clearly indicated by appropriate words his intention to be bound in some other capacity.

Section 64. Where a person, not otherwise a party to an instrument, places thereon his signature in blank before delivery, he is liable as indorser in accordance with the following rules:

1. If the instrument is payable to the order of a third person he is liable to the payee and to all subsequent parties.
2. If the instrument is payable to the order of the maker or drawer, or is payable to dearer, he is liable to all parties subsequent to the maker or drawer.
3. If he signs for the accommodation of the payee, he is liable to all parties subsequent to the payee.

Section 65. Every person negotiating an instrument by delivery or by a qualified endorsement, warrants:

1. That the instrument is genuine and in all respects what it purports to be.
2. That he has a good title to it.
3. That all prior parties had capacity to contract.
4. That he has no knowledge of any fact which would impair the validity of the instrument, or render it valueless.

But when the negotiation is by delivery only, the warranty extends in favor of no holder other than the immediate transferee.

The provisions of sub-division three of this section does not apply to persons negotiating public or corporate securities, other than bills and notes.

Section 66. Every endorser not an accommodating party who indorses without qualification, warrants to all subsequent holders in due course:

1. The matters and things mentioned in sub-division one, two, three and four of the next preceding section; and
2. That the instrument is at the time of his endorsement valid and subsisting.

And, in addition, every endorser engages that on due presentment, it shall be accepted or paid, or both, as the case may be, according to its tenor, and that if it be dishonored and the necessary proceedings on dishonor be duly taken he will pay the amount thereof to the holder, or to any subsequent endorser who may be compelled to pay it.

Section 67. Where a person places his endorsement on an instrument negotiable by delivery he incurs all the liabilities of an endorser.

Section 68. As respects one another, endorsers are liable *prima facie* in the order in which they indorse, but evidence is admissible to show that as between or among themselves they have agreed otherwise. Joint payees or joint endorsees who indorse are deemed to indorse jointly and severally.

Section 69. Where a broker or other agent negotiates an instrument without endorsement, he incurs all the liabilities prescribed by section sixty-five of this Act, unless he discloses the name of his principal, and the fact that he is acting only as agent.

- **Primary vs. Secondary Liability**: A person may be primarily liable if s/he agreed to pay the negotiable instrument.—The maker of a promissory note is primarily liable for paying the debt.
- A person who is secondarily liable is a contract guarantor and, under UCC Article 3, must pay the instrument only if the person who is primarily liable defaults on the obligation 33-4.
- **Acceptor and Drawee Liability:** The acceptor of a draft must pay the draft according to the terms at the time of acceptance (drawee's signed engagement to honor the draft as presented).
- A drawee has no liability on a check or draft unless it certifies or accepts it—In *Harrington v. MacNab*, the drawee bank had no liability to a payee for a drawer's insufficient funds.
- **Indorser Liability**: A person who indorses a negotiable instrument usually is secondarily liable – Indorsers are liable to each other in chronological order, from the last indorser back to the first

- To trigger secondary liability, the instrument must be properly presented for payment or acceptance, the instrument must be dishonored, and notice of the dishonor must be given to the person secondarily liable 33-6.
- **Discharge of Indorser Liability:** An indorser is discharged from liability if:—A bank accepts a draft after indorsement [3–415(d)] – Notice of dishonor is required and proper notice is not given to the indorser [3–415(c)]—No one presents a check or gives it to a depositary bank for collection within 30 days after the date of an indorsemen.
- **Signing an Instrument:** No person is contractually liable for negotiable instrument unless s/he or an authorized agent has signed it—Signature is binding on the represented person – Signature can be any name, word, or mark used in place of a written signature. *Marion T, LLC v. Northwest Metals Processors, Inc.*: if an agent or a representative signs negotiable instrument on behalf of someone else, agent should indicate clearly that signature was representative of someone else.
- **Presentment of a Note:** Since the maker of a note is primarily liable to pay it when due, dishonor occurs if the maker does not pay amount due when: 2) it is presented in the case of (a) a demand note or (b) a note payable at or through a bank on a definite date and presented on or after that date, or 3) if it is not paid on the date payable in the case of a note payable on a definite date (but not payable at or through a bank).
- **Presentment of a Draft or Check:** To obtain payment or acceptance on a draft or check, holder must present it to drawee by any commercially reasonable means—Written, oral, or electronic, Drawee obligated when it accepts (certifies).
- **Warranty Liability:** Person who transfers negotiable instrument or presents it for payment may have liability for implied warranties of presentment or transfer—Bank One, *N.A. v. Streeter:* Person who deposited checks to his account on which the payee's name had been altered breached transfer warranties and was not entitled to enforce the instruments.
- **Mistake in Payment or Acceptance:** Revised Article 3 follows general rule that payment or acceptance is final in favor of a holder in due course or payee who changes position in reliance on payment or acceptance—Bank bears burden of mistake 33-14.

Other Liability Rules

Negligence: A person who writes a negotiable instrument so as to invite alteration may not use the alteration or lack of authorization as a reason for not paying a person that in good faith pays the instrument or takes it for value [3–406] 33-15.

Imposter rule: An impostor convinces a drawer to make a check payable to the person impersonated or an organization the person claims to represent. UCC makes any endorsement "substantially similar" to that of named payee effective.

Fictitious payee rule: If someone writes a check to a fictitious payee, UCC allows any endorsement in the name of the fictitious payee to be effective as payee's endorsement in favor of any person that pays instrument in good faith or takes it for value or for collection.

Fraudulent endorsements by employees: Revised Article 3 specifically addresses employer liability for fraudulent endorsements by employees, adopting rule that the risk of loss for indorsements by employees entrusted with responsibilities for instruments (primarily checks) should fall on employer rather than the bank that takes the check or pays it [3–405] 33-18.

Victory Clothing Co., Inc. v. Wachovia Bank, N.A. Facts and Decision:—Employee engaged in double forgery of checks and a depositary bank allowed forger to deposit the checks to her own personal account, violating its own banking procedures and rules Employer sued bank for negligence—Court applied comparative negligence principles to split the loss between the company (30%) and the bank (70%).

Conversion: Revised Article 3 provides that the law applicable to conversion of personal property applies to instruments 33-20.

3.3 HOLDER AND HOLDER IN DUE COURSE

3.3.1 Holder

According to the Negotiable Instruments Act, 1881, Section 8,

> "Holder means any person entitled in his own name to the possession thereof and to receive or recover the amount due thereon from the parties thereto."

The '*Holder*' of a promissory note, bill of exchange, or cheque means the payee or indorsee who is in possession of it or the bearer thereof and does not include a beneficial owner claiming through a "benamder".

A person is called the holder of a negotiable instrument, if the following conditions are satisfied:

- He must be entitled to the possession of the instrument in his own name and under a legal title. Actual possession of the instrument is not essential; the holder must have the legal right to possess the instrument in his own name.
  For example, if a person acquires a cheque or bill by theft, fraud, or forged endorsement or finds it lying somewhere, he does not acquire in his own name legal title thereto and hence he can not be called its holder.
- He must be entitled to receive or recover the amount from the parties concerned in his own name. In case of an order instrument, it is essential that the name of the holder appears on the document as its Payee or endorsee. But in case of bearer instrument the name of the bearer is not essential to be appeared. In case a bill, note or cheque is lost or destroyed, the person who was entitled to receive payment at the time the instrument was lost, will continue to be regarded as its Holder, the finder does not become its holder.

3.3.2 Holder in Due Course

Holder in Due Course is an individual who takes a negotiable instrument for value, in good faith, with the belief that it is valid, with no knowledge of any defects.

According to the Negotiable Instruments Act, 1881, Section 9,

> "Holder in due course means any person who, for consideration, became the possessor of a promissory note, bill of exchange or cheque, if payable to bearer, or the payee or endorsee thereof if payable to order, before the amount mentioned in it became payable, and without having sufficient cause to believe that defect existed in the title of the person from whom he derived his title."

The Holder in Due Course (HDC) doctrine is a rule in commercial law that protects a purchaser of debt, where the purchaser is assigned the right to receive the debt payments.

A person becomes a holder in due course of a negotiable

instrument if the following conditions are satisfied:

1. The negotiable instrument must be in the possession of the holder in due course.
2. The negotiable instrument must be complete and regular on the face of it.
3. The instrument must have been obtained for valuable consideration, i.e., by paying its full value.
4. A holder in due course must have become a holder of the instrument before the date of its maturity. He must be entitled to transfer it. The instrument must have been obtained before it is matured.
5. The holder in due course must obtain the instrument without having sufficient cause to believe that any defect existed in the title of the transferor. He must be a holder of the instrument in good faith.
6. He must be valid holder of the instrument.
7. He should be entitled to sue in case of refusal of payment.

3.4 PRIVILEGES OF HOLDER IN DUE COURSE

Following are the important privileges which are enjoyed by the holder in due course.

1. Better Title

A holder in due course gets better title than the transferor while a holder cannot get a better title.

Example: Mr. Senha obtains an instrument by fraud he cannot sue it. If he transfers it to Mr. Nehra which make Mr. Nehra a holder in due course, Mr. Nehra can sue on the instrument.

2. Privilege in Case of Inchoate Stamped Instruments (Sec. 20)

In the case of inchoate stamped instrument, if the holder or original payee fills more amount than that was authorised, he cannot enforce the instrument for the whole amount (only actual authorised amount can be recovered).

If such an instrument is transferred to a holder in due course, he can claim the whole of the amount so entered provided that the amount is covered by the stamp affixed thereon. Thus, the defence that the amount filled by the holder was in excess of the authority given cannot be taken against a holder is due course.

3. Liability of Prior Parties

All prior parties to a negotiable instrument (i.e., its maker or drawer, acceptor and intervening indorsers) continue to remain liable to a holder in due course both jointly and severally (i.e., he can hold any or all prior parties liable) until the instrument is duly satisfied (Sec. 36). Whereas, only preceding party is liable to a succeeding party, if the succeeding party is only a holder.

4. Privilege in Case of Fictitious Bills (Sec. 42)

When a bill of exchange is drawn in a fictitious name and is made payable to the drawer's order (i.e., where both drawer and payee of a bill are fictitious persons), the bill is said to be a fictitious bill. Such a bill is not a good bill but the acceptor of a such bill is liable to the holder in due course.

5. Free from All Defects

As the instrument passes through the hands of a holder in due course to the subsequent holders, it becomes free from all defects.

6. Estoppel against Denying Original Validity of Instrument (Sec. 120)

The plea of original invalidity of the instrument; e.g., that no consideration actually passed between the maker and the payee of a promissory note; cannot be put forth against the holder in due course by the drawer of a bill of exchange or cheque or by the maker of a promissory note or by an acceptor of a bill for the honour of the drawer.

However, the parties are not precluded from challenging the validity of the instrument on the ground that at the time of making the instrument he was a minor or his signature had been forged or the instrument is otherwise void *ab-initio*, e.g., where a promissory note is made 'payable to bearer' it is void and illegal as per the Reserve Bank of India Act.

7. Estoppel against Denying Capacity of Payee to Indorse

"No maker of a note and no acceptor of a bill payable to order shall, in a suit thereon by a holder in due course, be permitted to deny the payee's capacity, at the date of the note or the bill to indorse the same" (Sec. 121).

Thus, a holder in due course can claim payment in his own name despite the payee's incapacity to indorse the instrument. As per Section 51, only a 'holder' or a person in lawful possession of the instrument is competent to indorse. Accordingly, a person who got the instrument for a gambling debt or for unlawful consideration cannot negotiate the same.

However, the holder in due course enjoys a privilege in this regard and he gets a good title even if he holds a negotiable instrument endorsed by a person who got the instrument for unlawful consideration because Section 121 provides that as against a holder in due course, no maker of a note and no acceptor of a bill payable to order shall be permitted to deny the payee's capacity to indorse the same.

8. No Effect of Conditional Delivery

When one instrument is delivered for special purpose and not for the transfer of ownership, this does not affect the holder in due course. If it is negotiated liable on the instruments shall remain liable to him.

Basis of difference	*Holder*	*Holder in Due Course*
1. Consideration	The existence of consideration is not essential in case of a holder. For example, if a Cheque is issued to provide a gift or donation to a charitable trust, the trust becomes its holder not holder in due course.	A holder in due course obtains the instruments after paying its full value. For example if the tuition fee paid to a school or college is for a valuable consideration, the school or the college acquires the status of holder in due course.
2. Possession	In case of a holder neither actual possession nor any time limit within which it must be acquired is required.	The person entitled to be called holder in due course must become the possessor of the instrument before it became payable. For example, if a bill of exchange is payable on March 20, 2007, a person who possesses it before this date is entitled to be its holder in due course.
3. Defect in transferor's Title	The holder may or may not have knowledge of defect in transferor's title. So he does not get better title than the true owner.	The most important point of difference is that a holder in due course acquires an instrument without having sufficient cause to believe that any defect existed in the title of the transferor. For example: A debt is due from a partner of a firm to X. The partner endorses in favor of X a cheque drawn in favor of the

firm. The circumstances of the case give rise to doubt about the title of the partner to the cheque drawn in favor of the firm. If X satisfies himself about the partner's valid title to the cheque he becomes its holder in due course.

3.5 DIFFERENCE BETWEEN HOLDER AND HOLDER IN DUE COURSE

From the definitions of the terms 'holder' and 'holder in due course' we may derive the following points of difference between them:

3.6 HOLDER FOR VALUE

The negotiable instruments act does not define the term "holder for value". In England, according to the bills of exchange act, where value of a bill has at any time been given, its holder is deemed to be a holder for value as regards the acceptor and all parties to the bill who became parties prior to such time. The person, who claims himself as the holder for value, need not himself give value. It may be given by prior party.

3.7 PAYMENT IN DUE COURSE

The payment of a negotiable instrument should be made to the right person by the paying banker or the acceptor of the bill; otherwise the latter shall be responsible for the same. The Negotiable Instruments Act provides protection to the paying banker or the drawee of a bill, provided the payment is made as required in the Act. Such payment is called 'payment in due course'.

According to the Negotiable Instrument Act, 1881, Section 10, "payment in due course means payment in accordance with the apparent tenor of the instrument in good faith and without negligence to any person in possession thereof under circumstances which do not afford a reasonable ground for believing that he is not entitled to receive payment of the amount therein mentioned."

The Essential Features of a Payment in Due Course are as follows:

1. The payment should be made in accordance with the apparent tenor of the instrument.

2. The payment should be made in good faith and without negligence.
3. Payment must be made to person who has the actual possession of the instrument. Person making the payment must insist on seeing the instrument before payment and obtain its delivery to him on payment.
4. Payment should not be made under circumstances which afford reasonable ground for believing that the person was not entitled to receive the amount mentioned in the instrument.

Some Related Issues

Bearer: Bearer means a person who by negotiation comes into possession of a negotiable instrument, which is payable to bearer.

Defective Title: A person who receives an instrument which has been lost or by means of fraud or any other unlawful means is not entitled to receive the amount due thereon unless he claims as holder in due course.

Liability of the Drawer: The drawer of the negotiable instrument will remain responsible to the payee till it is paid-off.

Liability of Prior Parties to Holder in Due Course: Every prior party to a negotiable instrument is liable thereon to a holder in due course until the instrument is duly satisfied.

3.8 CONCLUSION

1. Holder means any person entitled in his own name to the possession thereof and to receive or recover the amount due thereon from the parties thereto.
2. A holder in due course is one possessing a check or promissory note, given in return for something of value, who has no knowledge of any defects or contradictory claims to its payment. Such a holder is entitled to payment by the maker of the check or note.
3. Difference Between Holder and Holder in Due Course.

From the definitions of the terms 'holder' and 'holder in due course' we may derive the following points of difference between them:

1. Consideration
2. Possession
3. Defect in the transferor's title

SHORT QUESTIONS

1. Define Partial endorsement.
2. What is Restrictive endorsement?
3. What is Conditional endorsement?
4. Define Negotiation back.
5. Define Forged instruments.
6. Define Allonage.
7. Differentiate between holder and holder in due course.

LONG QUESTIONS

1. Explain clearly what is meant by negotiation? How is it affected and how does it differ from an ordinary assignment? Can an overdue instrument be negotiated?
2. State concisely the essential features of an instrument which makes it negotiable and specify the points of difference between the assignably and negotiability of such instruments.
3. A negotiable instrument may be transferred by negotiation and assignment, but with different consequences to the holder. Explain and illustrate.
4. Define the term endorsement. What are the various classes of endorsement?
5. Discuss the rules regarding negotiation of a lost instrument, a forged instrument, an instrument obtained by fraud, or for unlawful consideration.
6. Explain the rule that in the case of negotiable instrument forgery conveys no title. Mention the exceptions if any to this rule under Indian law.
7. The failure of consideration for negotiable instrument either total or partial is material only between immediate parties to the instrument. Comment.
8. Write short notes on:
   (a) Partial endorsement
   (b) Restrictive endorsement
   (c) Conditional endorsement
   (d) Negotiation back
   (e) Forged instruments
   (f) Allonage
9. "Partial endorsement does not operate as a Negotiation of the Instrument." Comment.

PRACTICAL PROBLEMS

Attempt the following problems, giving reasons for your answers:

1. A sells a radio to M, a minor, who pays for it by his cheque. A indorses the cheque to B, who takes it in good faith and for value. The cheque is dishonoured on presentation. Can B enforce payment of the cheque against A or M?
   [*Hint:* B can enforce payment of the cheque against A only (Sec. 26).]
2. A executed a promissory note in favour of B. Without B's demanding payment. A paid the money due on the note to B but left the note in his hands. Subsequently, B indorsed the note to C for consideration. C had knowledge of the payment made by A. C brings a suit against A and B for recovery of money on the note. Will he succeed against either or both?
   [*Hint:* C can enforce payment against either A or both (Secs. 9 and 58).]
3. A gives a blank acceptance to one Banerjee who fills it up as a bill payable to the drawer's order and himself signs it as the drawer and the first indorser in a fictitious name 'Jogender Lall'. Is A or Banerjee liable to the holder of the bill?
   [*Hint:* Both A and Banerjee are liable to the holder of the bill (Secs. 41 and 42). Moreover, the acceptance in the instant case is blank and such the instrument becomes payable to bearer. The right of the holder of the bill, therefore, will not be affected even if there is an indorsement in the name of fictitious person.]
4. A contracts to supply 100 fountain pens of a certain brand to B at Rs. 5 per pen. B executes a promissory note for Rs. 500 in favour of A for the price. After the pens have been delivered, B finds that one-fourth of the pens are damaged and unmerchantable. In a suit by A against B on the note, B claims a set-off of Rs. 200 for the damaged pens. Is he entitled to do so?
   [*Hint:* No, as the failure of consideration cannot be ascertained without a collateral inquiry (Sec. 45).]
5. A draws on B a bill payable three months after sight, it passé through several hands before X becomes its holder. On presentation by X, B refuses to accept. Discuss the rights of X on the bill.
   [*Hint:* All parties prior to X continue to be liable to X (Sec. 36).]
6. M draws a cheque in favour of N, a minor. N indorses it in favour of P, who on turn indorses it in favour of Q. The cheque is

dishonoured by the bank. Examine the rights of P and Q. Against whom can these rights be exercised?

[*Hint:* P has the right to recover payment of the cheque from M only. Q can hold both P and M liable for payment of the cheque (Sec. 26).]

7. A, on attaining the age of majority, executes a fresh promissory note in consideration of a promissory note executed by him during his minority. Can a suit be maintained on the fresh promissory note?

   [*Hint:* No, as the fresh promissory note is void for want of consideration.]

8. The director of a company borrowed Rs. 10,000 from A and executed a promissory note in favour of A. On the promissory note, there was no indication if the money was borrowed for and on behalf of the company. The company used the money for its purposes. Can the company be held liable to repay the loan on the basis of the promissory note?

   [*Hint:* No, the director is personally liable (Sec. 28).]

9. A bill of exchange purports to be drawn by A on B and is accepted by B. The bill is payable to C or order. C negotiates it to D who takes it as a holder in due course. In a suit by D on the bill, can B disclaim liability on ground that A's signature is forged?

   [*Hint:* No. (Sec.120).]

10. A signs his name on a bank but stamped instrument. He gives the paper to B with authority to fill it up as a promissory note for Rs. 250 only. B fraudulently fills the paper for Rs. 1,000, the stamp put upon it being sufficient to cover the amount. He then hands it to H for Rs. 1,000 who takes it without notice of fraud. Is A bound to pay Rs. 1,000 to H?

    [*Hint:* Yes (*Lloyds Bank Ltd. v. Cooke*, (1907) 1 K.B. 794; (Sec. 20).]

11. B obtains A's acceptance to a bill by fraud. B indorses it to C who takes it as a holder in due course. C indorses the bill to D who knows of the fraud. Can D recover from A?

    [*Hint:* Yes, D can recover the amount from A as he derived his title from C who is a holder in due course. Moreover, D is not a party to the fraud. Once the title has been cleansed of the defect, notwithstanding notice of the fraud, D gets a good title [*Guildford Trust v. Gloss*, (1926) 43 T.L.R. 167; Sec. 53).]

12. A bill is addressed to Herbert Morris who is a partner in the firm of "Perkin and Parker". Herbert Morris accepts the bill in the firm's name. Explain whether he will be personally liable on the bill or not.

    [*Hint:* Herbert Morris is personally liable on the bill as acceptor [*Nicholls v. Diamond*, (1853) 9 Ex. 184].

4

Discharge of Parties from Liability

LEARNING OBJECTIVES

4.1 Meaning of "Discharge"
4.2 Discharge of Negotiable Instruments
4.3 Discharge of Party Secondarily Liable
4.4 Discharge of Parties from Liability
4.5 Discharge by Operation of Law
4.6 Discharge by Operation of Law is not Included
4.7 Conclusion

4.1 MEANING OF "DISCHARGE"

According to Sec. 110. Meaning of Term "Discharge" is "**A contract is discharged when it loses Its force and effect as a legal obligation**".

A discharged contract is one which for some reason is no longer in force. It has lost its former legal effect. A paper may express a promise to pay money, yet the promise may be without any life in it, and not be expressive of any legal obligation. This may be true because the promise has been performed, or for other reasons that we will note.

4.2 DISCHARGE OF NEGOTIABLE INSTRUMENTS

(1) By payment in Due Course by or for the Principal Debtor

Payment by the maker or acceptor is the most usual method of discharging a note or bill. Assuming that there are no accommodation parties, but that the party primarily liable on the paper pays it when it becomes mature or after its maturity this discharges it and it thereafter becomes only so much waste paper so far as any legal obligation is concerned. One who pays such paper ought, of course, as a matter of ordinary precaution, to see that it is cancelled and given to him. And we have seen that one who pays negotiable paper must take care that he is paying it to the holder.

- In order to discharge the instrument, the payment must be a payment in due course, and second, a payment made by the principal debtor.
- If payment is made before the date of maturity, the instrument is not discharged as the payment is not in due course.
- Where payment is made by a party who is not a primary obligor or an accommodation party, his payment only conceals his own liability and those who are obligated after him. All prior parties primarily or secondarily liable on the bill, are liable to such a payer, and the payer may cancel indorsements subsequent to his own and reissue the paper, and it will be valid as against the prior parties.

If a party secondarily liable upon an instrument pays it, the instrument is not discharged.

(2) Payment by Accommodated Party

The real debtor may not be the maker or acceptor. One may have become maker of a note or acceptor of a bill for the accommodation of another, that is, in order to lend him credit. Such accommodator is liable just as a surety or guarantor is liable, although the creditor may know it is not really his debt. In such a case it is the real debtor's duty to pay the debt and if the accommodating party pays it, he may sue the party whom he has accommodated. If the real debtor pays the instrument, then it is discharged.

(3) By Intentional Cancellation by Holder

If a cancellation is by the holder with the intention of destroying the instrument, as such, it destroys it, but if the cancellation is unintentional, or under a mistake or by anyone without authority, the instrument is not destroyed.

(4) By acquisition of the Instrument by the Principal Debtor, at or after Maturity

If one makes a note and at or after its maturity buys it from the holder that is the same thing as paying it so far as discharging the instrument is concerned.

(5) Material Alteration

If an Instrument is altered in any material respect it releases all parties who did not authorize or assent thereto except that an Innocent purchaser for value may enforce it as it was before the alteration.

Payment by Third Persons

- If payment is made by a third person, the instrument is not discharged because payment is not made by the person principally liable.
- Not any one who desires may pay the instrument and then recover of the maker. He must be a person who has in some way made himself liable for the payment of the instrument.
- *Exception:* Where an instrument has been protested and someone voluntarily makes payment supra protest or for honor. And if the instrument was to give money in payment, the instrument is discharged.

4.3 DISCHARGE OF PARTY SECONDARILY LIABLE (Sec. 112)

A party secondarily liable is discharged (1) by an act that discharges the instrument; (2) by intentional cancellation of his signature by the holder; (3) by a valid tender of payment by a prior party; (4) by release of the principal debtor without express reservation of right against party secondarily liable; (5) by extension of time of payment without reserving right against the party secondarily liable; (6) by failure of the holder to take the proper steps to hold him.

A party secondarily liable is discharged by a failure of a holder, as we have seen, to take the proper steps to fix his liability. In such a case the instrument itself is not discharged; it still continues as a bill, note or check as the case may be, and the parties primarily liable may be sued upon it.

So in other ways a party secondarily liable may be discharged though the instrument continues in force. One is a valid tender of payment by a prior party. This does not discharge the instrument. One who owes money on a note is not allowed to escape his liability if he may succeed in making a tender which is not accepted. Tender of money under a debt due must be kept good. But such tender does discharge a party secondarily liable. This debt is not really his. He is to be held only in case the party does not pay who ought to pay. Consequently, his rights are strictly guarded and if a tender is made to such holder which such holder ought to have accepted, such secondary party may say that he will not be held for a failure of the party primarily liable to pay when the holder might once have had payment of his debt.

Such tender, however, must be a valid tender. A tender in something not "legal tender," or a tender of the wrong amount or a tender before the instrument was due, would not be good tenders, and would not discharge.

If the holder releases the principal debtor this will discharge the party secondarily liable, unless at the time the release is made there is an express reservation made by the holder of his rights against the party secondarily liable.

The same may be said of a contract to extend the time of payment. A mere failure to sue, or a mere unenforceable agreement, which is too indefinite to amount to a contract or is without consideration, and which therefore could not be enforced by the debtor, would not release the party secondarily liable, if his liability had been duly fixed by the taking of the proper steps.

Effect of Payment by Party Secondarily Liable (Sec. 113)

A payment by a party secondarily liable does not discharge the Instrument, but such party is put in his former position and may assert his rights against prior parties, or again negotiate the paper.

A party secondarily liable may pay the paper without discharging it, because it yet has to be paid by the party primarily liable. Thus, suppose A makes a note to B, who indorses to C, who indorses to D. D being unable at maturity to secure payment by A, or any other party, C, in order to avoid suit, pays it. He now stands in the same situation as though he had not indorsed it, and may sue the prior parties as he could have done before indorsement. Or, striking out his indorsement to D, he may negotiate it to E, and thus make himself again secondarily liable if the instrument cannot be enforced by E.

Renunciation of Rights (Sec. 115)

A holder may expressly renounce his rights against any party either by so stating in writing or delivering up the Instrument.

One may renounce rights against any party or may renounce all rights upon the instrument. If he does so, the party or the instrument, as the case may be, is discharged. The discharge must be in writing, or in case of renunciation of rights against the principal debtor, it may be by delivery up of the instrument.

4.4 DISCHARGE OF PARTIES FROM LIABILITY

The maker, acceptor or endorser respectively of a negotiable instrument is discharged from liability thereon—

(1) If the party primarily liable pays the instrument in full, all parties on the instrument are discharged;
(2) If a secondarily liable party pays the instrument, only that party and subsequent parties are discharged—the primary party (maker or drawer), as well as any indorsers prior to the paying party, remain(s) liable;
(3) Intentional cancellation (e.g., writing "PAID" across the face of the instrument, destroying the instrument) discharges the liability of all parties;
(4) Material alteration may discharge the liability of any party(ies) affected by the alteration;
(5) A party reacquiring an instrument discharges the liability of all intervening indorsers to subsequent holders who are not holders in due course; and
(6) If a party's right of recourse (i.e., right to seek reimbursement) has been impaired, that party may be discharged from further liability.

Payment by Cheque or other Negotiable Paper

1. When they actually have been cashed, or
2. When, through the fault of the creditor, they have been impaired.

   Note: A creditor isn't bound to accept a check in satisfaction of his demand because a check, even if good when offered, doesn't meet the requirements of legal tender.

4.5 DISCHARGE BY OPERATION OF LAW (Sec. 120)

When persons secondarily liable on the instrument are discharged.—A person secondarily liable on the instrument is discharged:

(a) By any act which discharges the instrument;
(b) By the intentional cancellation of his signature by the holder;
(c) By the discharge of a prior party;
(d) By a valid tender or payment made by a prior party;
(e) By a release of the principal debtor unless the holder's right of recourse against the party secondarily liable is expressly reserved; and
(f) By any agreement binding upon the holder to extend the time of payment or to postpone the holder's right to enforce the instrument unless made with the assent of the party secondarily liable or unless the right of recourse against such party is expressly reserved.

4.6 DISCHARGE BY OPERATION OF LAW IS NOT INCLUDED

1. Discharge by reason of bankruptcy;
2. Discharge of a party not given due notice of dishonor; and
3. Discharge by the statute of limitations.

4.7 CONCLUSION

A discharged contract is one which for some reason is no longer in force. It has lost its former legal effect.

Negotiable instrument is discharged by:

- Payment in due source;
- Payment by accommodating party;
- Cancellation by debtor;
- Material alteration; and
- Acquisition of instrument by principle debtor.

A party is discharged from liabilities when—

- o If the party primarily liable pays the instrument in full, all parties on the instrument are discharged;
- o If a secondarily liable party pays the instrument, only that party and subsequent parties are discharged—the primary

party (maker or drawer), as well as any indorsers prior to the paying party, remain(s) liable;

- o Intentional cancellation (e.g., writing "PAID" across the face of the instrument, destroying the instrument) discharges the liability of all parties;
- o Material alteration may discharge the liability of any party(ies) affected by the alteration;
    - A party reacquiring an instrument discharges the liability of all intervening indorsers to subsequent holders who are not holders in due course; and
- o If a party's right of recourse (i.e., right to seek reimbursement) has been impaired, that party may be discharged from further liability.

TEST QUESTIONS

1. What are the various ways in which a contract may be discharged?
2. Write a note on discharge of a contract by consent?
3. Discuss fully the law relating to novation of contracts?
4. "Impossibility of performance is, as a rule, not an excuse for non-performance of a contract". Discuss.
5. Discuss the effects of supervening impossibility on the performance of a contract.
6. Does an impossibility which arises subsequent to the information of a contract excuse the promisor from performing the contract in all cases?
7. How far are liabilities of the parties to a contract affected by supervening impossibility?
8. Explain, with illustrations, what is meant by the frustration of the contract.
9. "If the frustration of a contract goes, either by the destruction of the subject-matter or by reason of such long interruption or delay that the performance is really in effect that of a different contract, and the parties have not provided what in that event is to happen, the performance of a contract is to be regarded as frustrated". – per Goddard, J., in *Tatem v. Gamboa* (1939) 1 K.B. 142. Explain and comment on this statement.
10. "The doctrine of frustration has often been said to depend on adding a term to the contract by implication". Comment.
11. Explain, breach of contract as a mode of discharge of contract.

12. What do you understand by 'anticipatory breach of contract'? State the rights of the promise in case of such breach.

PRACTICAL PROBLEMS

1. P let premises in Calcutta to D in January 1942, at a high rent for opening a restaurant, the agreement to remain in force as long as British European troops would remain stationed in Calcutta. Although British European troops continued to be stationed in the town, the particular locality of the restaurant was declared out of bounds for the troops and thus D lost their custom. D refused to pay P the dues of rent on the plea of frustration of contract. Advise P.
   [*Hint:* P can claim the rent from D as this case is not covered by supervening impossibility (*Sachindra Nath v. Gopal Chander*, A.I.R. (1949) Cal.]
2. In July 1989 Radhe Shyam entered into a contract with Raja Ram to build a house for a fixed sum of Rs. 10,00,000. Owing to unexpected shortage of skilled labour and of certain materials, the contract took 24 months to complete instead of the 12 months expected the cost about Rs. 1,50,000. Radhe Shyam contended that the contract had been frustrated and that he was entitled for the cost actually incurred. Advise Raja Ram.
   [*Hint:* The doctrine of supervening impossibility does not apply in the case. The present case is that of mere difficulty and not of impossibility.]
3. Is the promisor absolved from performing the contract in following cases:
   (a) A music hall was agreed to be let out on certain dates but before those days it was destroyed by fire.
   (b) An artist undertook to paint a picture for a certain price, but before he could do so, he met with an accident and lost his eye-sight.
   (c) A entered into a contract with B on 1st March for the supply of certain imported goods in the month of September of the same year. In June, by an Act of Parliament, the import of such goods was banned.
   (d) A contracts to marry B, being already married to C, and being forbidden by the law to which he is subject to practice polygamy.

(e) A promises B, for valuable consideration, to put back the life of a dead relation of B by some supematural powers but fails to keep up his promise.

(f) A agreed to sell to B the entire crop of apples growing in his field. After the agreement was made a sudden frost destroyed the crop.

[*Hint:* Yes, as the contract is or becomes void in all the cases on the ground of initial or supervening impossibility due to: (a) destruction of subject matter (*Taylor v. Caldwell*). (b) disablement of one of the parties (Robinson v. Davison). (c) subsequent illegality (*Baily v. De Crespigny*). (d) Illegality (Para 3 of Sec. 56). (e) initial impossibility of performance (Para 1 of Sec. 56). (f) supervening impossibility (*Howel v. Coupland*).]

4. A owned a room in a hotel which was hired to B for watching the coronation procession of King Edward II, at £ 141 payable at the time of the contract. £ 100 were paid in cash. But before the balance was paid, the procession was cancelled. B filed a suit for the recovery of the amount he had paid. Decide.

[*Hint:* B can recover £ 100 were paid in cash and is not bound to pay the balance £ 41. But if A has incurred some expense in partial performance of the contract, he can claim compensation from B].

5. A contract between G and R provided that "60 bales are to be given to you by me; I shall go on supplying goods to you of the Victoria Mills as soon as they are supplied to me by the said mill". R failed to deliver the goods as agreed. In a suit for damages for non-delivery of goods, R pleaded impossibility on the ground that the goods were not supplied to him by the mill. Advise G.

[*Hint:* G is entitled to claim damages for the non-delivery of goods by R (*Ganga Saran v. Ram Charan*)].

6. A shipbuilder contracted to build and supply a ship of specified dimensions according to a model to be approved by the buyers, it being a term of the contract that the ship was to carry a certain dead weight on a certain draught. The model was approved and it was subsequently found to be a mathematical impossibility to produce a ship which would fulfil the terms of the contract. Can the shipbuilder plead impossibility of performance in suit against him by the buyer?

[*Hint:* Yes (Para 1 of Sec. 56)].

7. The unloading of a ship was delayed beyond the date agreed with the shipowners owing to a strike of dock labourers. On a suit by shipowners for damages, the plea of impossibility of performance was raised. Advise the shipowners.
   [*Hint:* The shipowners can claim damages.]
8. A enters into a contract with B signing at his theatre for three nights for a fee of Rs. 100 for every night. She signs for two nights and is taken ill. (a) Can B ask for damages for loss of profit from A? (b) Would your answer be different if A signs for the theatre another night?
   [*Hint:* (a) No (Sec. 56). (b) No.]

5

DISHONOUR OF NEGOTIABLE INSTRUMENT

LEARNING OBJECTIVES

5.1 Introduction
5.2 Dishonour of Negotiable Instrument
5.3 Effect of Dishonour
5.4 Consequences of not giving Notice of Dishonour
5.5 Conclusion

5.1 INTRODUCTION

If negotiable instrument is presented for acceptance, sight or payment before the acceptor, maker, drawer or other party liable thereon by or on behalf of the holder but such persons refused to accept it or to make payment upon it. A negotiable instrument is said to be dishonoured when the drawee refuse to accept it or not make payment. In such situation a notice of dishonour must be given to the drawee under the negotiable instrument act a person is entitled for compensation without giving the notice of dishonour in some cases.

5.2 DISHONOUR OF NEGOTIABLE INSTRUMENT

A negotiable instrument may be dishonoured by (i) non-acceptance, (ii) non-payment.

1. Dishonour by Non-acceptance

A bill of exchange is said to be dishonoured, by non-acceptance in the following cases:

1. When the drawee or one of the several drawees (not being partners) makes default in acceptance upon being required to accept the bill (48 hours required).
2. Where the presentment for acceptance is excused and the bill is not accepted.
3. Where the drawee is incompetent to contract.
4. Where the drawee makes the acceptance qualified.
5. If the drawee is fictitious person or after reasonable search cannot be found.

2. Dishonour by Non-payment

A promissory note, bill of exchange or cheque is said to be dishonoured by non-payment when the maker, acceptor of the bill or drawee of the cheque makes default in payment upon being duly required to pay the same. (Sec. 92)

Also, a promissory note or bill of exchange is dishonoured by non-payment when presentment for payment is excused expressly by the maker of the note or acceptor of the bill and PN or BE remains unpaid.

5.3 EFFECT OF DISHONOUR

As soon as a negotiable instrument is dishonoured (either by non-acceptance or by non-payment) the holder becomes entitled to sue the parties liable to pay thereon.

- The holder MUST, however, give notice of dishonour to all the parties against whom he intends to proceed.

Notice of Dishonour

- Notice of dishonour means formal communication of the fact of dishonour.
- Such a notice also serves the purpose of enabling the person so notified to protest himself against the prior parties.

Notice by Whom

- Notice of dishonour must be given by the holder or by some party to the instrument who remain liable thereon.
- Any party receiving the notice of dishonour must also transmit the same to all prior parties in order to make them liable to him.
- No suit can be filed against the prior party if he has not transmitted the fact of dishonour of instrument.
- One person can give the notice only.
- Duly authorised person can also give notice.

Notice to Whom

- Notice of dishonour must be given to all parties (other than the maker of note, acceptor of a bill or drawee of a cheque) to whom the holder seeks to make liable or other duly authorised agents.
- In case of death of a person, notice must be given to his legal representative and were he has been declared insolvent to his Official Assignee.
- In case after dispatch of notice and before it receipt the person dies, it will be treated as if the notice has been served. (Not knowing the fact).

Mode of Giving Notice

- It may be oral or in writing. If it is in writing it must be sent by post.
- It should be given in reasonable time.

What is Reasonable Time?

In determining what is reasonable time the consideration is to be given:

1. Nature of the instrument.
2. The usual course of dealing with respect to similar instruments.
3. Distance between the parties.
4. While calculating public holidays shall be excluded.
5. In case a party received the notice of dishonour is to transmit the same to his prior parties, the transmission should be done in reasonable time.

When Notice of Dishonour is Unnecessary

1. Where the indorsee while signing in that capacity adds the words 'notice of dishonour waived'.
2. Where the drawer of a cheque countermanded payment.
3. Where the party charged could not suffer damage for want of notice such as bank account closed or in case of accommodation bill.
4. Where the party to whom the notice is to be given not traceable or the party who has to give notice is unable to give notice like death, accident or serious illness.
5. When the drawer also happens to be acceptor.
6. In case the Promissory Note which is not negotiable.
7. When the party entitled to receive notice promise to pay unconditionally the amount as due after due date.

5.4 CONSEQUENCES OF NOT GIVING NOTICE OF DISHONOUR

Any party to negotiable instrument (other than maker of a note, acceptor of a bill or drawer of cheque) is discharged from his obligation under the instrument unless circumstances are such where no notice is required to be sent.

Noting

- In case a promissory note or bill of exchange has been dishonoured by non-acceptance or non-payment notice, the holder may cause such dishonour to be noted by Notary Public.
- Noting must be made within reasonable time after dishonour and must specify: (i) the date of dishonour, (ii) the reason assigned for dishonour, and (iii) the notary's charges.

Protest

"Protest" is a formal certificate issued by the notary public to the holder of the bill or note on his demand (noting is merely a record of dishonour on the instrument).

Contents of Protest

1. The instrument itself or a literal transcript of the instrument and of every thing written or printed thereon.

2. The name of the person for whom and against whom the instrument has been protested.
3. The fact and reason for dishonour.
4. The place and time of dishonour.
5. The signature of notary public.
6. In case of acceptance for honour or payment for honour, the names of the persons by whom and for whom it is accepted or paid.

Compensation for Dishonor of Negotiable Instruments (Section 117)

Section 117 in The Negotiable Instruments Act, 1881 states some rules as to compensation.—The compensation payable in case of dishonour of a promissory note, bill of exchange or cheque, by any party liable to the holder or any indorsee, shall be determined by the following rules:—

- The holder is entitled to the amount due upon the instrument together with the expenses properly incurred in presenting, noting and protesting it;
- When the person charged resides at a place different from that at which the instrument was payable, the holder is entitled to receive such sum at the current rate of exchange between the two places;
- An endorser who, being liable, has paid the amount due on the same is entitled to the amount so paid with interest at 2[eighteen per centum] per annum from the date of payment until tender or realization thereof, together with all expenses caused by the dishonour and payment;
- When the person charged and such endorser reside at different places, the endorser is entitled to receive such sum at the current rate of exchange between the two places;
- The party entitled to compensation may draw a bill upon the party liable to compensate him, payable at sight or on demand, for the amount due to him, together with all expenses properly incurred by him. Such bill must be accompanied by the instrument dishonoured and the protest thereof (if any). If such bill is dishonoured, the party dishonouring the same is liable to make compensation thereof in the same manner as in the case of the original bill.

Dishonour of Cheque (Section 138: Negotiable Instruments Act, 1881)

Section 138 of Negotiable Instruments Act Provides some rules in case of dishonor of a cheque that are as follows:

- Dishonour of cheque for insufficiency, etc., of funds in the account:

  Where any cheque drawn by a person on an account maintained by him with a banker for payment of any amount of money to another person from out of that account for the discharge, in whole or in part, of any debt or other liability, is returned by the bank unpaid, either because of the amount of money standing to the credit of that account is insufficient to honour the cheque or that it exceeds the amount arranged to be paid from that account by an agreement made with that bank, such person shall be deemed to have committed an offence and shall, without prejudice to any other provision of this Act, be punished with imprisonment for a term which may extend to two years, or with fine which may extend to twice the amount of the cheque, or with both:

  Provided that nothing contained in this section shall apply unless—

  (a) the cheque has been, presented to the bank within a period of six months from the date on which it is drawn or within the period of its validity, whichever is earlier;

  (b) the payee or the holder in due course. of the cheque as the case may be, makes a demand for the payment of the said amount of money by giving a notice, in writing, to the drawer of the cheque, within thirty days of the receipt of information by him from the bank regarding the return of the cheque as unpaid; and

  (c) the drawer of such cheque fails to make the payment of the said amount of money to the payee or, as the case may be, to the holder in due course of the cheque, within fifteen days of the receipt of the said notice.

  Explanation. For the purposes of this section, "debt or other liability" means a legally enforceable debt or other liability.

Ingredients of Offence under Section 138

1. The cheque should have been issued for the discharge, in whole or part, of any debt or other liability.

2. The cheque should have been presented within a period of six months or within its validity period whichever is earlier.
3. The payee or holder in due course should have issued a notice in writing to the drawer within 30 days of the receipt of information by him from the Bank regarding the return of the cheque as unpaid.
4. After receipt of the said notice from the holder in due course, the drawer should have failed to pay the cheque within 15 days of receipt of the said notice.

Grounds for Dishonour of Cheque

"Funds Insufficient"

Section 138 describes the above ground of insufficient funds in the account of the drawer of the cheque in the following words:

The amount of money standing to the credit of the account of the drawer on which the cheque is drawn is insufficient to honour the cheque, or

> The cheque amount exceeds the amount that can be paid by the bank under an arrangement entered into between the bank and the drawer of the cheque.

However, besides the above, the Courts have also accepted some other heads which though expressly do not say 'insufficient funds' but are implied to mean the same and a cheque dishonoured on any of these grounds can be used for the purpose of prosecution under section 138 Negotiable Instruments Act. Some of theses grounds are:

1. Account Closed: "It is an offence under section 138 of the Act—Closure of account would be an eventuality after the entire amount in the account is withdrawn—It means that there was no amount in the credit of 'that account' on the relevant date when the cheque was presented for honouring the same".

This has been held by the Hon'ble Supreme Court of India in—

> *Neps Micon Ltd. and others vs. Magma Leasing Ltd., 1999 ISJ (Banking) 0433; 1999 (1) Apex C.J. 0624; 1999, AIR (SCW) 1637*

2. 'Stop Payment' Instructions: "Once the cheque has been drawn and issued to the payee and the payee has presented the cheque, 'stop payment' instructions will amount to dishonour of cheque."

Mahendr S. Dadia vs. State of Maharashtra, I (1999) Banking Cases (BC) 133 (17/03/1998)

3. 'Refer to drawer': "...makes out a case under section 138 of the Negotiable Instruments Act, 1881 which expression means that there were not sufficient funds with the bank in the account of the respondent"

Lily Hire Purchase Ltd. vs. Darshan Lal, (1997) 89 Company Cases 663 (10/01/1997)

4. 'Not a clearing member': "Cheque returned with endorsement 'not a clearing member'. To attract the provisions of section 138 NI Act, the cheque should be presented with the bank on which it I drawn—If the cheque is not presented to the bank on which it is drawn, then provisions of Sec. 138 would not be attracted. If bank on which the cheque is drawn is not a clearing member of the Reserve Bank of India—unpaid return of the cheque would not attract section 138."

Chairman, Jawahar Cooperative Urban Bank Ltd. and others vs. Ramanjaneya Enterprises, Hyd. and Another, 2005 (5) Criminal Reported Judgements (CRJ) 0591; 2005 (2) Dishonour of Cheque Reporter (DCR) 0169

5. Effect of other endorsements: It has been repeatedly held by courts that manifest dishonest intention of the drawer resulting in dishonour of the cheque would lead to prosecution under section 138 Negotiable Instruments Act regardless of the actual ground of dishonour.

Cases when notice of dishonour is unnecessary: Notice of dishonour is unnecessary in the following cases:

(i) When it is dispensed with by the party entitled to notice.
(ii) In order to charge the drawer, when he has countermanded payment.
(iii) When the party charged could not suffer damage for want of notice.
(iv) When the party entitled to notice can not after due search, be found.
(v) To charge the drawers, when the acceptors is also a drawer.
(vi) In case of promissory note.
(vii) When after knowing the facts, the party entitled to notice promises to pay unconditionally.

5.5 CONCLUSION

Dishonor of Negotiable Instruments may occur in two cases:

- Dishonour by Non-Acceptance
- Dishonour by Non-Payment

As soon as a negotiable instrument is dishonoured (either by non-acceptance or by non-payment) the holder becomes entitled to sue the parties liable to pay thereon.

The holder MUST, however, give notice of dishonour to all the parties against whom he intends to proceed.

Notice of dishonour must be given to all parties (other than the maker of note, acceptor of a bill or drawee of a cheque) to whom the holder seeks to make liable or other duly authorised agents.

Noting and Protesting should be done by the holder to record the fact of Dishonour.

The holder is entitled to compensation on dishonour of the instrument according to section 117 of the Negotiable Instrument Act, 1881.

Where any cheque is dishonoured by the bank for insufficiency of the funds in the account of the person drawing the cheque, such person shall be deemed to have committed an offence and shall be punished with imprisonment for a term which may extend to two years, or with fine which may extend to twice the amount of the cheque, or with both.

TEST QUESTIONS

1. In what different ways may a negotiable instrument be dishonoured? What are the duties of holder of a dishonoured bill?
2. How and when should a notice be served on a bill being dishonoured by either non-acceptance or non-payment? Under what circumstances is notice of dishonour unnecessary?
3. When are bills of exchange, promissory notes or cheques said be dishonoured? Who should give notice of dishonour and to whom?
4. What is the difference between discharge of negotiable instrument and discharge of a party to a negotiable instrument? When is negotiable instrument said to be discharged? Give examples.
5. What are the various ways in which one or more parties to a negotiable instrument is? Are discharged from liability? Discuss.
6. In what manner is the liability of a drawer, acceptor and endorser of a negotiable instrument discharged?

7. Explain the meaning of material alteration in a negotiable instrument. What is the effect of such alteration?

PRACTICAL PROBLEMS

1. A draws on B bill payable three months after sight. It passes through several hands before X becomes its holder on presentation by X refuses to pay. Discuss the rights of X on the bill.

   [*Hint:* X is entitled to recover money on the bill from all the prior parties. A, the drawer of the oil, and B the accepter of the bill, are layable to X as principal debtors whereas the intervening indorsers are liable as sureties].

2. Is notice of dishonor A necessary in the following cases:

   (a) A having the balance of Rs. 100 at his bankers and having no authority to overdraw, draws a cheque for Rs. 500.

   The cheque is dishonoured when duly presented for payment.

   (b) A the drawer of a bill informs H, the holder of the bill, that the bill will be dishonoured on presentment.

   [*Hint:* Notice is dishonor to A is not necessary in both the cases].

6

NEGOTIATION AND ENDORSEMENT

LEARNING OBJECTIVES

6.1 Introduction—Negotiation
6.2 Modes of Negotiation
6.3 Assignment
6.4 Endorsement
6.5 Negotiation Back
6.6 Conclusion

6.1 INTRODUCTION—NEGOTIATION

Negotiation may be defined as the process by which a third party is constituted the holder of the instrument so as to entitle him to the possession of the same and to receive the amount due thereon in his own name. According to section 14 of the Act, 'when a promissory note, bill of exchange or cheque is transferred to any person so as to constitute that person the holder thereof, the instrument is said to be negotiated.' The main purpose and essence of negotiation is to make the transferee of a promissory note, a bill of exchange or a cheque the holder thereof.

Negotiation thus requires two conditions to be fulfilled, namely:

1. There must be a transfer of the instrument to another person; and

2. The transfer must be made in such a manner as to constitute the transferee the holder of the instrument. Handing over a negotiable instrument to a servant for safe custody is not negotiation; there must be a transfer with an intention to pass title.

6.2 MODES OF NEGOTIATION

Negotiation may be effected in the following two ways:

1. **Negotiation by delivery** (Sec. 47): Where a promissory note or a bill of exchange or a cheque is payable to a bearer, it may be negotiated by delivery thereof.

   Example: A, the holder of a negotiable instrument payable to bearer, delivers it to B's agent to keep it for B. The instrument has been negotiated.

2. **Negotiation by endorsement and delivery** (Sec. 48): A promissory note, a cheque or a bill of exchange payable to order can be negotiated only be endorsement and delivery.

   Unless the holder signs his endorsement on the instrument and delivers it, the transferee does not become a holder. If there are more payees than one, all must endorse it.

6.3 ASSIGNMENT

Bills, notes and cheques represent debts and as such have been held to be assignable without endorsement. Transfer by assignment takes place when the holder of a negotiable instrument sells his right to another person without endorsing it. The assignee is entitled to get possession and can recover the amount due on the instrument from the parties thereto. Of the two methods of transfer of negotiable instruments discussed, transfer by negotiation is recognized by the Negotiable Instrument Act.

Negotiation and Assignment Distinguished

The various points of distinction between negotiation and assignment are as below:

1. Negotiation requires delivery only to constitute a transfer, whereas assignment requires a written document signed by the transferor.

2. Consideration is always presumed in the case of transfer by negotiation. In the case of assignment consideration must be proved.
3. In case of negotiation, notice of transfer is not necessary, whereas in the case of assignment notice of the transfer must be given by the assignee to the debtor.
4. The assignee takes the instrument subject to all the defects in the title of the transferor. If the title of the assignor was defective the title of the assignee is also defective. However, in case of negotiation the transferee takes the instrument free from all the defects in the title of the transferor. A holder in due course is not affected by any defect in the title of the transferor. He may therefore have a better title than the transferor.
5. In case of negotiation a transferee can sue the third party in his own name. But an assignee cannot do so.

Importance of Delivery in Negotiation

Delivery is a voluntary transfer of possession from one person to another. Delivery is essential to complete any contract on a negotiable instrument whether it be contract of making endorsement or acceptance. The property in the instrument does not pass unless the delivery is fully completed. Section 46 of the Act provides that a negotiable instrument is not made or accepted or endorsed unless it is delivered to a proper person. For instance, if a person signs a promissory note and keeps it with himself, he cannot be said to have made a promissory note; only when it is delivered to the payee that the promissory note is made. Delivery may be actual or constructive. Delivery is actual when it is accompanied by actual change of possession of the instrument. Constructive delivery is effected without any change of actual possession.

6.4 ENDORSEMENT

The word 'endorsement' in its literal sense means, writing on the back of an instrument. But under the Negotiable Instruments Act it means, the writing of one's name on the back of the instrument or any paper attached to it with the intention of transferring the rights therein. Thus, endorsement is signing a negotiable instrument for the purpose of negotiation. The person who effects an endorsement is called an 'endorser', and the person to whom negotiable instrument is transferred by endorsement is called the 'endorsee'.

6.4.1 Essentials of a Valid Endorsement

The following are the essentials of a valid endorsement:

1. It must be on the instrument. The endorsement may be on the back or face of the instrument and if no space is left on the instrument, it may be made on a separate paper attached to it called allonage. It should usually be in ink.
2. It must be made by the maker or holder of the instrument. A stranger cannot endorse it.
3. It must be signed by the endorser. Full name is not essential. Initials may suffice. Thumb-impression should be attested. Signature may be made on any part of the instrument. A rubber stamp is not accepted but the designation of the holder can be done by a rubber stamp.
4. It may be made either by the endorser merely signing his name on the instrument (it is a blank endorsement) or by any words showing an intention to endorse or transfer the Instrument to a specified person (it is an endorsement in full). No specific form of words is prescribed for an endorsement. But intention to transfer must be present. When in a bill or note payable to order the endorsee's name is wrongly spelt, he should when he endorses it, sign the name as spelt in the instrument and write the correct spelling within brackets after his endorsement.
5. It must be completed by delivery of the instrument. The delivery must be made by the endorser himself or by somebody on his behalf with the intention of passing property therein. Thus, where a person endorses an instrument to another and keeps it in his papers where it is found after his death and then delivered to the endorsee, the latter gets no right on the instrument.
6. It must be an endorsement of the entire bill. A partial endorsement, i.e. which purports to transfer to the endorse a part only of the amount payable does not operate as a valid endorsement. If delivery is conditional, endorsement is not complete until the condition is fulfilled.

6.4.2 Who may Endorse?

The payee of an instrument is the rightful person to make the first endorsement. Thereafter, the instrument may be endorsed by any person who has become the holder of the instrument. The maker or the drawer cannot endorse the instrument but if any of them has become the holder thereof he may endorse the instrument. (Sec. 51). The maker or drawer cannot endorse or negotiate an instrument unless he is in lawful possession of instrument or is the holder thereof. A payee or endorsee cannot endorse or negotiate unless he is the holder thereof.

6.4.3 Classes of Endorsement

An endorsement may be:

(1) Blank or general.
(2) Special or full.
(3) Partial.
(4) Restrictive.
(5) Conditional.

(a) Blank or general endorsement (Sections 16 and 54): It is an endorsement when the endorser merely signs on the instrument without mentioning the name of the person in whose favour the endorsement is made. Endorsement in blank specifies no endorsee. It simply consists of the signature of the endorser on the endorsement. A negotiable instrument even though payable to order becomes a bearer instrument if endorsed in blank. Then it is transferable by mere delivery. An endorsement in blank may be followed by an endorsement in full.

Example: A bill is payable to X. X endorses the bill by simply affixing his signature. This is an endorsement in blank by X. In this case the bill becomes payable to bearer. There is no difference between a billor note indorsed in blank and one payable to bearer. They can both be negotiated by delivery.

(b) Special or full endorsement (Section 16): When the endorsement contains not only the signature of the endorser but also the name of the person in whose favour the endorsement is made, then it is an endorsement in full. Thus, when endorsement is made by writing the words "Pay to A or A's order," followed by the signature of the endorser, it is an endorsement in full. In such an endorsement, it is only the endorsee who can transfer the instrument.

Conversion of endorsement in blank into endorsement in full: When a person receives a negotiable instrument in blank, he may without signing his own name, convert the blank endorsement into an endorsement in full by writing above the endorser's signature a direction to pay to or to the order of himself or some other person. In such a case the person is not liable as the endorser on the bill. In other words, the person transferring such an instrument does not incur all the liabilities of an endorser. (Section 49).

Example: A is the holder of a bill endorsed by B in blank. A writes over B's signature the words "Pay to C or order." A is not liable as endorser but the writing operates as an endorsement in full from B to C. Where a bill is endorsed in blank, or is payable to bearer and is afterwards endorsed by another in full, the bill remains transferable by delivery with regard to all parties prior to such endorser in full. But such endorser in full cannot be sued by anyone except the person in whose favour the endorsement in full is made. (Section 55).

(c) **Partial endorsement (Section 56)**: A partial endorsement is one which purports to transfer to the endorsee a part only of the amount payable on the instrument. Such an endorsement does not operate as a negotiation of the instrument.

Example: A is the holder of a bill for Rs. 1000. He endorses it "pay to B or order Rs. 500." This is a partial endorsement and invalid for the purpose of negotiation.

(d) Restrictive endorsement (Section 50): The endorsement of an instrument may contain terms making it restrictive. Restrictive endorsement is one which either by express words restricts or prohibits the further negotiation of a bill or which expresses that it is not a complete and unconditional transfer of the instrument but is a mere authority to the endorsee to deal with bill as directed by such endorsement. "Pay C," "Pay C for my use," "Pay C for the account of B" are instances of restrictive endorsement. The endorsee under a restrictive endorsement acquires all the rights of the endorser except the right of negotiation.

(e) Conditional or qualified endorsement: Negotiation means the transfer of a check, promissory note, bill of exchange or other negotiable instrument to another for money, goods, services or other benefit. It is open to the endorser to annex some condition to his owner liability on the endorsement. An endorsement where the endorsee limits or negatives his liability by putting some condition in the instrument is called a conditional endorsement. A condition imposed by the endorser may be a condition precedent or a condition subsequent. An endorsement which says that the amount will become payable if the endorsee attains majority embodies a condition precedent. A conditional endorsement unlike the restrictive endorsement does not affect the negotiability of the instrument. It is also some times called qualified endorsement. An endorsement may be made conditional or qualified in any of the following forms:

(i) **'Sans recourse' endorsement**: An endorser may be express word exclude his own liability thereon to the endorser or any subsequent holder in case of dishonour of the instrument. Such an endorsement is called an endorsement sans recourse (without recourse). Thus, 'Pay to A or order sans recourse, 'pay to A or order without recourse to me,' are instances of this type of endorsement. Here if the instrument is dishonoured, the subsequent holder or the endorsee cannot look to the endorser for payment of the same.

An agent signing a negotiable instrument may exclude his personal liability by using words to indicate that he is signing as agent only. The same rule applies to directors of a company signing instruments on behalf of a company. The intention to exclude personal liability must be clear. Where an endorser so excludes his liability and afterwards becomes the holder of the instrument, all intermediate endorsers are liable to him.

Example: A is the holder of a negotiable instrument. Excluding personal liability by an endorsement without recourse, he transfers the instrument to B, and B endorses it to C, who endorses it to A. A can recover the amount of the bill from B and C.

(ii) **Facultative endorsement**: An endorsement where the endorser extends his liability or abandons some right under a negotiable instrument, is called a facultative endorsement. "Pay A or order, Notice of dishonour waived" is an example of facultative endorsement.

(iii) **'Sans frais' endorsement**: Where the endorser does not want the endorsee or any subsequent holder, to incur any expense on his account on the instrument, the endorsement is 'sans frais'.

(iv) **Liability dependent upon a contingency:** Where an endorser makes his liability depend upon the happening of a contingent event, or makes the rights of the endorsee to receive the amount depend upon any contingent event, in such a case the liability of the endorser will arise only on the happening of that contingent event. Thus, an endorser may write 'Pay A or order on his marriage with B'. In such a case, the endorser will not be liable until the marriage takes place and if the marriage becomes impossible, the liability of the endorser comes to an end.

Effects of Endorsement

The legal effect of negotiation by endorsement and delivery is:

(i) To transfer property in the instrument from the endorser to the endorsee.
(ii) To vest in the latter the right of further negotiation, and
(iii) A right to sue on the instrument in his own name against all the other parties

Cancellation of Endorsement

When the holder of a negotiable instrument, without the consent of the endorser destroys or impairs the endorser's remedy against prior party, the endorser is discharged from liability to the holder to the same extent as if the instrument had been paid at maturity (Section 40).

6.5 NEGOTIATION BACK

'Negotiation back' is a process under which an endorsee comes again into possession of the instrument in his own right. Where a bill is re-endorsed to a previous endorser, he has no remedy against the intermediate parties to whom he was previously liable though he may further negotiate the bill.

Instruments without Consideration

A person cannot pass a better title than he himself possesses. A person who is a mere finder of a lost goods or a thief or one who obtains any article by fraud or for an unlawful consideration does not get any title to the thing so acquired. The true owner can recover it not only from him but from any person to whom he may have sold it. But there is a difference between the transfer of ordinary goods and negotiation of negotiable instruments. The Negotiable Instruments Act provides protection to those persons who acquire the instruments in good faith and for valuable consideration. A holder in due course who has no means to discover the defect of title in an instrument of any previous holder when the instrument may have passed through several hands must be protected if he obtains the instrument for value and in good faith. Section 58 of the Act provides that no person in possession of an instrument with a defect of title can claim the amount of the instrument unless he is a holder in due course. The moment an instrument comes into the hands of a holder in due course, not only does he get a title which is free from all defects, but having passed through his hands the instrument is cleaned of all defects.

Lost Instruments

Where the holder of a bill or note loses it, the finder gets no title to it. The finder cannot lawfully transfer it. The man who lost it can recover it from the finder. But if the instrument is transferable by mere delivery and there is nothing on its face to show that it does not belong to the finder, a holder obtaining it from the finder in good faith and for valuable consideration and before maturity is entitled to the instrument and can recover payment from all the parties thereof. If the instrument is transferable by endorsement, the finder cannot negotiate it except by forging the endorsement. The holder of the instrument when it is lost must give a notice of loss to all the parties liable on it and also a public notice by advertisement. The holder of a lost bill remains owner in law and as such on maturity can demand payment from the acceptor, and if is dishonoured he must give notice of dishonour to prior parties. The owner of the lost bill has a right to obtain the duplicate from the drawer and on refusal he can sue the drawer for the same.

Stolen Instrument

The position of thief of an instrument is exactly the same as that of a finder of lost instruments. A thief acquires no title to an instrument if he receives payment on it the owner can sue him for the recovery of the amount. But if an instrument payable to bearer is stolen and if transferred to a holder in due course, the owner must suffer.

Instruments obtained by Fraud

It is of the essence of all contracts including those on negotiable instruments, that they must have been brought about by free consent of the parties competent to contract. Any contract to which consent has been obtained by fraud is voidable at the option of the person whose consent was so obtained. A person who obtains an instrument by fraud gets a defective title. But if such an instrument passes into the hands of a holder in due course, the plea of fraud will not be available against him. If however, it could be shown that a person without negligence on his part was induced to sign an instrument it being represented to him to be a document of a different kind he would not be liable even to a holder in due course.

Instrument obtained for an Unlawful Consideration

The general rules as to the legality of object or consideration of a contract apply to contracts on negotiable instruments also. An instrument given for an illegal consideration is void and does not covey a valid title to the holder. He cannot enforce payment against any party thereto. Thus, a bill of exchange given in consideration of future illicit cohabitation is void. But if such an instrument passes into the hands of a holder in due course, he obtains a good and complete title to it.

Forged Instrument

Forgery confers no title and a holder acquires no title to a forged instrument. A forged instrument is treated as a nullity. Forgery with the intention of obtaining title to an instrument would include:

(1) Fraudulently writing the name of an existing person,
(2) Signing the name of a fictitious person with the intention that it may pass that of a real person, or
(3) Signing one's own name with the intention that the signature may pass as the signature of some other person of the same name.

Examples:

(a) On a note for Rs.1000, A forges B's signature to it as maker. C, a holder who takes it *bona-fide* and for value acquires no title to the note.

(b) On a bill for Rs.1000 A's acceptance to the bill is forged. The bill comes into hands of B, a *bona-fide* holder for value, B acquires no title to the bill.

Forged Endorsement

The case of a forged endorsement is slightly different. If an instrument is endorsed in full, it cannot be negotiated except by an endorsement signed by the person to whom or to whose order the instrument is payable, for the endorsee obtains title only through his endorsement. If an endorsement is forged, the endorsee acquires no title to the instrument even if he is a *bona-fide* purchaser. On the other hand, if the instrument is a bearer instrument or has been endorsed in blank, and there is a forged endorsement the holder gets a good title because holder in such a case derives title by delivery and not by endorsement. Bankers are specially protected against forged endorsement under section 85 of the Act.

Examples:

(a) A bill is endorsed, "Pay X or order." X must endorse the bill and if his signature is forged, the bill is worthless.

(b) A bill is payable to "X or order." It is stolen from X and the thief forges X's endorsement and endorses it to Y who takes it in good faith and for value. Y acquires no title to the bill.

Instrument without Consideration

Sections 43 to 45 of the Negotiable Instrument Act deal with the consequences of failure or absence of consideration in negotiable instruments. In the case of negotiable instruments consideration is presumed to exist between the parties unless the contrary is proved. As between immediate parties, if an instrument is made, drawn or endorsed without consideration, or for a consideration which subsequently fails, it is void. As between immediate parties, failure of consideration has the same effect as the absence of consideration. For instance, if a promissory note is delivered by the maker to the payee as a gift, it cannot be enforced against such maker.

Examples:

(a) C the holder of a bill endorses it in blank to D receiving no value. D for value transfers it by delivery to E. E is a holder of value.

(b) A is the holder of a bill for consideration. A endorses it to B, without consideration. The property in the bill passes to B. The bill is dishonoured at maturity. B cannot sue A on the bill. As between remote parties, the defence of absence or failure of consideration is not available at all. The holder in due course who has paid consideration can recover it from all prior parties immaterial of the fact whether any of them has received consideration or not. Where there is a partial absence or failure of consideration, as between immediate parties, only that part can be recovered which was actually paid. However, a holder in due course is not affected by this rule. But even between immediate parties, where the part of the consideration which is absent or cannot be ascertained without collateral inquiry, the whole of the amount is recoverable.

Examples: (a) A owes B Rs. 500. B draws a bill on A for Rs. 1000. A to accommodate B and at his request accepts it. If B sues A on the bill he can only recover Rs. 500. (b) A draws a bill on B for Rs. 500 payable to the order A. B accepts the bill but subsequently dishonours it by non-payment. A sues B on the bill. B proves that it was accepted for value as to Rs. 400 and as an accommodation to A (the plaintiff) for Rs. 100. A can only recover Rs. 400. But if this bill gets into the hands of a holder in due course, he can recover the full amount of Rs. 500.

6.6 CONCLUSION

- Negotiation may be defined as the process by which a third party is constituted the holder of the instrument so as to entitle him to the possession of the same and to receive the amount due thereon in his own name.
- Two modes of Negotiation: By deliver; By delivery and endorsement.
- Transfer by assignment takes place when the holder of a negotiable instrument sells his right to another person without endorsing it.
- Endorsement means, the writing of one's name on the back of the instrument or any paper attached to it with the intention of transferring the rights therein. Thus, endorsement is signing a negotiable instrument for the purpose of negotiation.
- An endorsement may be:

  (1) Blank or general.
  (2) Special or full.
  (3) Partial.

(4) Restrictive.
(5) Conditional.

- Instruments issued without consideration are void and can not be enforced.

SHORT QUESTIONS

1. What is Negotiation?
2. Who can endorse?
3. What is Partial Endorsement?
4. Define Restrictive Endorsement.
5. What do you mean by Conditional endorsement.
6. Define Negotiation back.
7. Define Forged instruments.
8. Define Allonage.

LONG QUESTIONS

1. Explain clearly what is meant by negotiation? How is it effected and how does it differ from an ordinary assignment? Can an overdue instrument be negotiated?
2. State concisely the essential features of an instrument which makes it negotiable and specify the points of difference between the assignability and negotiable of such instruments.
3. A negotiable instrument may be transferred by negotiation and assignment, but with different consequences to the holder. Explain and illustrate.
4. Define the term 'endorsement'. What are the various classes of endorsement?
5. Discuss the rules regarding negotiation of a lost instrument, a forged instrument, an instrument obtained by fraud, or for unlawful consideration.
6. Explain the rule that in the case of negotiation instrument forgery conveys no title. Mention the exceptions if any to this rule under Indian law.
7. The failure of consideration for negotiable instrument either total or partial is material only between immediate parties to the instrument. Comment.
8. Write short notes on:
   (a) Partial endorsement
   (b) Restrictive endorsement

(c) Conditional endorsement
(d) Negotiation back
(e) Forged instruments
(f) Allonage.

9. "Partial endorsement does not operate as a negotiation of the instrument". Comment.

PRACTICAL PROBLEMS

Attempt the following problems, giving reasons for your answer:

1. A drew cheques in favour of B. A's clerk forged B's endorsement and negotiated the cheques to C who took them in good faith and for value. C received payment of the cheques. A claims to recover the amount from C, will he succeed?
[*Hint:* In his claim to recover the amount from C, A will succeed if the cheque was an order cheque, but fail if the cheque was payable to bearer.]
2. A, the holder of a bill, indorses it 'sans recours' to B, B indorses it to C to D, D to E and E indorses it again to A. can A recover the amount of the bill from B, C, D or E or any of them ?
[*Hint:* Yes. A recover the amount of the bill from B, C, D or E or any of them (Sec. 52).]
3. A, the payee-holder of a bill, indorsed it in blank and delivered it to B. B also indorsed it in blank and delivered it to C. C indorsed it in full to D or order. D without endorsement delivered it to E. What are E's right and against whom ?
[*Hint:* E, as the bearer of the instrument, is entitled to receive payment from the drawer, the acceptor, A or B but not C and D (Sec. 5).]
4. A executes a promissory note in favour of B for Rs. 2,500. B receives the amount from C and makes endorsement thus: "Received the amount due under this promissory note from C" and "signs it and hands it over to C." Can C maintain a suit on the promissory note?
[*Hint:* No, he can however sue B for return of his money.]
5. A, the holder of a bill, transfer it to B as payable to him or his order for the express purpose that it shall be discounted. B indorses it to C who takes it *bona-fide* and for value. Discuss the position of C as against A and B.
[*Hint:* C can hold both A and B liable for the payment of the bill (Sec. 46).]

6. A draws a bill on B who accepts it without consideration. He indorses the bill to C for valuable consideration. On due date when C presents the bill to B for payment, B contends absence of consideration. Decide the case giving reasons.
   [*Hint:* B is liable to pay on the bill to C who is a holder in due course (Sec. 43).]
7. A bill is payable to 'A or order'. It is stolen from A and the thief forges A's signature endorses it to B who takes it as a holder in due course. Can B recover upon the bill? Give reasons for your answer.
   [*Hint:* No, B cannot recover upon the bill (Sec. 58).]
8. A owes B rate 1,000. He makes a promissory note for the amount payable to B. A dies and the note is afterwards found among his papers and delivers B. Can B sue upon the note? Give reason for your answer.
   [*Hint:* A No, D cannot sue upon the note (Sec. 46).]
9. A Promissory note is executed by A in favour of B in consideration of C, A relation of B, forbearing to sue C on a prior promissory note executed by A in favour of B any lawful consideration.
   [*Hint:* Yes. Sec. 2(d) of the Indian Contract Act, 1872.]
10. A accepted a bill and gave it to B who put his name as a drawer for the purpose for discounting it and paying the proceeds to A, B, having failed to discount, returned the bill to A who, intending to cancel it, tore it into two and three and the pieces into the street. B picked up the pieces pasted them together and put the bill into circulation. Examine the liability of A on the bill.
    [*Hint:* A is not liable on the bill as he did not deliver the bill to B (Sec. 46).]
11. A, the holder of a bill, transfers it to B without consideration. B also transfers it to C without consideration C transfers it to D for value. D transfers it to E, without consideration. Discuss the rights of E against A, B, C and D.
    [*Hint:* E can recover the amount of the bill from A, B and C not from the D (Sec. 43).]
12. A agrees to supply a quantity of paper to B. B accepts a bill for Rs. 1,000 drawn by A being the price of the paper. The paper deliver to B. But it turns out to be not of the quality stipulated for and is worth Rs. 500 only. B retain the paper. Can A recover from B the full amount of the note?
    [*Hint:* Yes, A can recover the full amount of the note (Sec. 45).]

13. A bill is indorsed: 'pay X or order'. X indorses the bill in blank. It comes into the hands of A, who passes it by simple delivery to B. B forges A's endorsement and transfers it to C. Can sue any of the parties to the bill? Would there be any difference if the bill stolen from X custody and the thief forges X Endorsement and transfers it for value without notice to C?
[*Hint:* C can sue all the prior parties as he drives his title not through the forged endorsement of the, but through the genuine endorsement of X. If X endorsement by the thief, C cannot hold the prior parties liable.]
14. A owes to B Rs. 500 for which he makes a promissory note payable to B. He cuts the note to halves for safe transmission and sends one half by post to B. Afterwards before he sends the other to B, he changes in mind and asks he to return to him the part already sent to him. B, however, asks for the other half of the promissory note. Decide the case.
[*Hint:* Delivery is not complete in this case. A can ask for the return of the part which has already deliver to B (Sec. 46).]
15. A bill is drawn payable to 'A or order'. A loses the bill and B, who find it forges A signature and indorses it to C who takes it for value and in good faith. Examine right of C.
[*Hint:* C gets no title to the bill as it is negotiated by means of a forged endorsement.]
16. A draws a bill on B for Rs. 500 payable to his order. A accepts the bill subsequently dishonours it by non-payment. A sues B on the bill. B proves that it was accepted for value as to Rs. 400 and as accommodation to A as to the balance. How much can A recover from B?
[*Hint:* A can recover only Rs. 400 from B (Sec. 44).]
17. A draws for his own accommodation a bill Rs.1000 on B, and after acceptance by B, indorses it to C as security for Rs. 500. B is adjudged insolvent. Discuss the rights of C.
[*Hint:* C can recover Rs. 500 from A (Sec. 44).]
18. A draws a bill of exchange on B, payable to C or order, C indorses it in blank and negotiated it. The bill is thereafter lost and X, who finds it forges endorsement in blank of D and negotiate it by delivery to E. discuss if E as any rights on the instrument and if so, against whom.
[*Hint:* E has the right to sue all parties prior to him.]

19. B obtains A's acceptances to a bill by fraud. He indorses it to see who takes it as a holder in due course. C indorses the bill to D who knows of the fraud. Can D recover from A?
[*Hint:* No. D cannot recover as he had knowledge of the fact that B had obtained A's acceptance to the bill by fraud (Sec. 43).]
20. D gets a bill exchange on which there are three earlier endorsements by A, B and C. discuss the rights of D, if any, on the bill: (a) if B's endorsement is bill in goods faith without notice, (b) if the signature of the drawer is forged.
[*Hint:* (a) D will acquire title to the bill if the earlier endorsement by A to B is blank, (b) signature of A, the drawer is forged the instrument is a null and forgery passes no title to B, C or D.]

7

THE INFORMATION TECHNOLOGY ACT, 2008

LEARNING OBJECTIVES

7.1 Introduction
7.2 Definitions
7.3 Digital Signature
7.4 Electronic Governance
7.5 Attribution, Acknowledgment and Despatch of Electronic Records
7.6 Secure Electronic Records And Secure Digital Signatures
7.7 Regulation of Certifying Authorities
7.8 Digital Signature Certificates
7.9 Duties of Subscribers
7.10 Penalties and Adjudication
7.11 The Cyber Regulations Appellate Tribunal
7.12 Technical Aspects
7.13 Offences
7.14 Prevention of Fraud

7.1 INTRODUCTION

The Information Technology Amendment Act, 2008 (IT Act, 2008) is a substantial addition to India's Information Technology Act

(ITA-2000). The IT Amendment Act was passed by the Indian Parliament in October 2008 and came into force a year later. The Act is administered by the Indian Computer Emergency Response Team.

The original Act was developed to promote the IT industry, regulate e-commerce, facilitate e-governance and prevent cybercrime. The Act also sought to foster security practices within India that would serve the country in a global context. The Amendment was created to address issues that the original bill failed to cover and to accommodate further development of IT and related security concerns since the original law was passed.

Changes in the Amendment include: redefining terms such as "communication device" to reflect current use; validating electronic signatures and contracts; making the owner of a given IP address responsible for content accessed or distributed through it; and making corporations responsible for implementing effective data security practices and liable for breaches.

PRELIMINARY

1. Short title, extent, commencement and application.—(1) This Act may be called the Information Technology Act, 2000.

(2) It shall extend to the whole of India and, save as otherwise provided in this Act, it applies also to any offence or contravention thereunder committed outside India by any person.

(3) It shall come into force on such date as the Central Government may, by notification, appoint and different dates may be appointed for different provisions of this Act and any reference in any such provision to the commencement of this Act shall be construed as a reference to the commencement of that provision.

(4) Nothing in this Act shall apply to,—

(a) a negotiable instrument as defined in section 13 of the Negotiable Instruments Act, 1881;

(b) a power-of-attorney as defined in section 1A of the Powers-of-Attorney Act, 1882;

(c) a trust as defined in section 3 of the Indian Trusts Act, 1882;

(d) a will as defined in clause (h) of section 2 of the Indian Succession Act, 1925 including any other testamentary disposition by whatever name called;

(e) any contract for the sale or conveyance of immovable property or any interest in such property;
(f) any such class of documents or transactions as may be notified by the Central Government in the Official Gazette.

7.2 DEFINITIONS

2. Definitions.—(1) In this Act, unless the context otherwise requires,—

(a) "**access**" with its grammatical variations and cognate expressions means gaining entry into, instructing or communicating with the logical, arithmetical, or memory function resources of a computer, computer system or computer network;
(b) "**addressee**" means a person who is intended by the originator to receive the electronic record but does not include any intermediary;
(c) "**adjudicating officer**" means an adjudicating officer appointed under sub-section (1) of section 46;
(d) "**affixing digital signature**" with its grammatical variations and cognate expressions means adoption of any methodology or procedure by a person for the purpose of authenticating an electronic record by means of digital signature;
(e) "**appropriate Government**" means as respects any matter,-
  (i) Enumerated in List II of the Seventh Schedule to the Constitution; and
  (ii) relating to any State law enacted under List III of the Seventh Schedule to the Constitution,

  the State Government and in any other case, the Central Government;
(f) "**asymmetric crypto system**" means a system of a secure key pair consisting of a private key for creating a digital signature and a public key to verify the digital signature;
(g) "**Certifying Authority**" means a person who has been granted a licence to issue a Digital Signature Certificate under section 24;
(h) "**Certification practice statement**" means a statement issued by a Certifying Authority to specify the practices that the

Certifying Authority employs in issuing Digital Signature Certificates;

(i) **"Computer"** means any electronic magnetic, optical or other high-speed data processing device or system which performs logical, arithmetic, and memory functions by manipulations of electronic, magnetic or optical impulses, and includes all input, output, processing, storage, computer software, or communication facilities which are connected or related to the computer in a computer system or computer network;

(j) **"Computer network"** means the interconnection of one or more computers through—

  (i) the use of satellite, microwave, terrestrial line or other communication media; and

  (ii) terminals or a complex consisting of two or more interconnected computers whether or not the interconnection is continuously maintained;

(k) **"Computer resource"** means computer, computer system, computer network, data, computer data base or software;

(l) **"Computer system"** means a device or collection of devices, including input and output support devices and excluding calculators which are not programmable and capable of being used in conjunction with external files, which contain computer programmes, electronic instructions, input data and output data, that performs logic, arithmetic, data storage and retrieval, communication control and other functions;

(m) **"Controller"** means the Controller of Certifying Authorities appointed under sub-section (1) of section 17;

(n) **"Cyber Appellate Tribunal"** means the Cyber Regulations Appellate Tribunal established under sub-section (1) of section 48;

(o) **"Data"** means a representation of information, knowledge, facts, concepts or instructions which are being prepared or have been prepared in a formalised manner, and is intended to be processed, is being processed or has been processed in a computer system or computer network, and may be in any form (including computer printouts magnetic or optical storage media, punched cards, punched tapes) or stored internally in the memory of the computer;

(p) **"Digital signature"** means authentication of any electronic record by a subscriber by means of an electronic method or procedure in accordance with the provisions of section 3;

(q) "**Digital Signature Certificate**" means a Digital Signature Certificate issued under sub-section (4) of section 35;

(r) "**Electronic form**" with reference to information means any information generated, sent, received or stored in media, magnetic, optical, computer memory, micro film, computer generated micro fiche or similar device;

(s) "**Electronic Gazette**" means the Official Gazette published in the electronic form;

(t) "**Electronic record**" means data, record or data generated, image or sound stored, received or sent in an electronic form or micro film or computer generated micro fiche;

(u) "**Function**", in relation to a computer, includes logic, control arithmetical process, deletion, storage and retrieval and communication or telecommunication from or within a computer;

(v) "**Information**" includes data, text, images, sound, voice, codes, computer programmes, software and databases or micro film or computer generated micro fiche;

(w) "**Intermediary**" with respect to any particular electronic message means any person who on behalf of another person receives, stores or transmits that message or provides any service with respect to that message; and

(x) "**Key pair**", in an asymmetric crypto system, means a private key and its mathematically related public key, which are so related that the public key can verify a digital signature created by the private key.

7.3 DIGITAL SIGNATURE

3. Authentication of electronic records.—(1) Subject to the provisions of this section any subscriber may authenticate an electronic record by affixing his digital signature.

(2) The authentication of the electronic record shall be effected by the use of asymmetric crypto system and hash function which envelop and transform the initial electronic record into another electronic record.

Explanation.—For the purposes of this sub-section, "hash function" means an algorithm mapping or translation of one sequence of bits into another, generally smaller, set known as "hash result" such that an electronic record yields the same hash result every time the algorithm is executed with the same electronic record as its input making it computationally infeasible—

(a) to derive or reconstruct the original electronic record from the hash result produced by the algorithm;

(b) that two electronic records can produce the same hash result using the algorithm.

(3) Any person by the use of a public key of the subscriber can verify the electronic record.

(4) The private key and the public key are unique to the subscriber and constitute a functioning key pair.

7.4 ELECTRONIC GOVERNANCE

4. Legal recognition of electronic records.—Where any law provides that information or any other matter shall be in writing or in the typewritten or printed form, then, notwithstanding anything contained in such law, such requirement shall be deemed to have been satisfied if such information or matter is—

(a) rendered or made available in an electronic form; and

(b) accessible so as to be usable for a subsequent reference.

5. Legal recognition of digital signatures.—Where any law provides that information or any other matter shall be authenticated by affixing the signature or any document shall be signed or bear the signature of any person then, notwithstanding anything contained in such law, such requirement shall be deemed to have been satisfied, if such information or matter is authenticated by means of digital signature affixed in such manner as may be prescribed by the Central Government. *Explanation.*—For the purposes of this section, "signed", with its grammatical variations and cognate expressions, shall, with reference to a person, mean affixing of his hand written signature or any mark on any document and the expression "signature" shall be construed accordingly.

6. Use of electronic records and digital signatures in Government and its agencies.—(1) Where any law provides for—

(a) the filing of any form, application or any other document with any office, authority, body or agency owned or controlled by the appropriate Government in a particular manner;

(b) the issue or grant of any licence, permit, sanction or approval by whatever name called in a particular manner;

(c) the receipt or payment of money in a particular manner,

then, notwithstanding anything contained in any other law for the time being in force, such requirement shall be deemed to have been satisfied if such filing, issue, grant, receipt or payment, as the case may be, is effected by means of such electronic form as may be prescribed by the appropriate Government.

(2) The appropriate Government may, for the purposes of sub-section (1), by rules, prescribe—

(a) the manner and format in which such electronic records shall be filed, created or issued; and

(b) the manner or method of payment of any fee or charges for filing, creation or issue any electronic record under clause.

Retention of electronic records.—(1) Where any law provides that documents, records or information shall be retained for any specific period, then, that requirement shall be deemed to have been satisfied if such documents, records or information are retained in the electronic form, if—

(a) the information contained therein remains accessible so as to be usable for a subsequent reference;

(b) the electronic record is retained in the format in which it was originally generated, sent or received or in a format which can be demonstrated to represent accurately the information originally generated, sent or received; and

(c) the details which will facilitate the identification of the origin, destination, date and time of despatch or receipt of such electronic record are available in the electronic record:

Provided that this clause does not apply to any information which is automatically generated solely for the purpose of enabling an electronic record to be despatched or received.

(2) Nothing in this section shall apply to any law that expressly provides for the retention of documents, records or information in the form of electronic records

Publication of rule, regulation, etc., in Electronic Gazette—Where any law provides that any rule, regulation, order, bye-law, notification or any other matter shall be published in the Official Gazette, then, such requirement shall be deemed to have been satisfied if such rule, regulation, order, bye-law, notification or any other matter is published in the Official Gazette or Electronic Gazette:

Provided that where any rule, regulation, order, bye-law, notification or any other matter is published in the Official Gazette or Electronic Gazette, the date of publication shall be deemed to be the date of the Gazette which was first published in any form.

9. Sections 6, 7 and 8 not to confer right to insist document should be accepted in electronic form.—Nothing contained in sections 6, 7 and 8 shall confer a right upon any person to insist that any Ministry or Department of the Central Government or the State Government or any authority or body established by or under any law or controlled or funded by the Central or State Government should accept, issue, create, retain and preserve any document in the form of electronic records or effect any monetary transaction in the electronic form.

10. Power to make rules by Central Government in respect of digital signature.—The Central Government may, for the purposes of this Act, by rules, prescribe—

(a) the type of digital signature;
(b) the manner and format in which the digital signature shall be affixed;
(c) the manner or procedure which facilitates identification of the person affixing the digital signature;
(d) control processes and procedures to ensure adequate integrity, security and confidentiality of electronic records or payments; and
(e) any other matter which is necessary to give legal effect to digital signatures.

7.5 ATTRIBUTION, ACKNOWLEDGMENT AND DESPATCH OF ELECTRONIC RECORDS

Attribution of electronic records—An electronic record shall be attributed to the originator—

(a) if it was sent by the originator himself;
(b) by a person who had the authority to act on behalf of the originator in respect of that electronic record; or
(c) by an information system programmed by or on behalf of the originator to operate automatically.

Acknowledgment of receipt.—(1) Where the originator has not agreed with the addressee that the acknowledgment of receipt of electronic record be given in a particular form or by a particular method, an acknowledgment may be given by—

(a) any communication by the addressee, automated or otherwise; or

(b) any conduct of the addressee, sufficient to indicate to the originator that the electronic record has been received.

(2) Where the originator has stipulated that the electronic record shall be binding only on receipt of an acknowledgment of such electronic record by him, then unless acknowledgment has been so received, the electronic record shall be deemed to have been never sent by the originator.

(3) Where the originator has not stipulated that the electronic record shall be binding only on receipt of such acknowledgment, and the acknowledgment has not been received by the originator within the time specified or agreed or, if no time has been specified or agreed to within a reasonable time, then the originator may give notice to the addressee stating that no acknowledgment has been received by him and specifying a reasonable time by which the acknowledgment must be received by him and if no acknowledgment is received within the aforesaid time limit he may after giving notice to the addressee, treat the electronic record as though it has never been sent.

Time and place of despatch and receipt of electronic record.—(1) Save as otherwise agreed to between the originator and the addressee, the dispatch of an electronic record occurs when it enters a computer resource outside the control of the originator.

(2) Save as otherwise agreed between the originator and the addressee, the time of receipt of an electronic record shall be determined as follows, namely:

(a) if the addressee has designated a computer resource for the purpose of receiving electronic records,

(i) receipt occurs at the time when the electronic record enters the designated computer resource; or

(ii) if the electronic record is sent to a computer resource of the addressee that is not the designated computer resource, receipt occurs at the time when the electronic record is retrieved by the addressee;

(b) if the addressee has not designated a computer resource along with specified timings, if any, receipt occurs when the electronic record enters the computer resource of the addressee.

(3) Save as otherwise agreed to between the originator and the addressee, an electronic record is deemed to be dispatched at the place where the originator has his place of business, and is deemed to be received at the place where the addressee has his place of business.

(4) The provisions of sub-section (2) shall apply notwithstanding that the place where the computer resource is located may be different from the place where the electronic record is deemed to have been received under sub-section (3).

(5) For the purposes of this section,—

(a) if the originator or the addressee has more than one place of business, the principal place of business shall be the place of business;

(b) if the originator or the addressee does not have a place of business, his usual place of residence shall be deemed to be the place of business; and

(c) "usual place of residence", in relation to a body corporate, means the place where it is registered.

7.6 SECURE ELECTRONIC RECORDS AND SECURE DIGITAL SIGNATURES

Secure electronic record.—Where any security procedure has been applied to an electronic record at a specific point of time, then such record shall be deemed to be a secure electronic record from such point of time to the time of verification.

Secure digital signature.—If, by application of a security procedure agreed to by the parties concerned, it can be verified that a digital signature, at the time it was affixed, was—

(a) unique to the subscriber affixing it;

(b) capable of identifying such subscriber; and

(c) created in a manner or using a means under the exclusive control of the subscriber and is linked to the electronic record to which it relates in such a manner that if the electronic record was altered the digital signature would be invalidated,

then such digital signature shall be deemed to be a secure digital signature.

Security procedure.—The Central Government shall for the purposes of this Act prescribe the security procedure having regard to commercial circumstances prevailing at the time when the procedure was used, including—

(a) the nature of the transaction;
(b) the level of sophistication of the parties with reference to their technological capacity;
(c) the volume of similar transactions engaged in by other parties;
(d) the availability of alternatives offered to but rejected by any party;
(e) the cost of alternative procedures; and
(f) the procedures in general use for similar types of transactions or communications.

7.7 REGULATION OF CERTIFYING AUTHORITIES

Appointment of Controller and other officers.—(1) The Central Government may, by notification in the Official Gazette, appoint a Controller of Certifying Authorities for the purposes of this Act and may also by the same or subsequent notification appoint such number of Deputy Controllers and Assistant Controllers as it deems fit.

(2) The Controller shall discharge his functions under this Act subject to the general control and directions of the Central Government.

(3) The Deputy Controllers and Assistant Controllers shall perform the functions assigned to them by the Controller under the general superintendence and control of the Controller.

(4) The qualifications, experience and terms and conditions of service of Controller, Deputy Controllers and Assistant Controllers shall be such as may be prescribed by the Central Government.

(5) The Head Office and Branch Office of the office of the Controller shall be at such places as the Central Government may specify, and these may be established at such places as the Central Government may think fit.

(6) There shall be a seal of the Office of the Controller.

Functions of Controller.—The Controller may perform all or any of the following functions, namely:

(a) exercising supervision over the activities of the Certifying Authorities;

(b) certifying public keys of the Certifying Authorities;
(c) laying down the standards to be maintained by the Certifying Authorities;
(d) specifying the qualifications and experience which employees of the Certifying Authorities should possess;
(e) specifying the conditions subject to which the Certifying Authorities shall conduct their business;
(f) specifying the contents of written, printed or visual materials and advertisements that may be distributed or used in respect of a Digital Signature Certificate and the public key;
(g) specifying the form and content of a Digital Signature Certificate and the key,
(h) specifying the form and manner in which accounts shall be maintained by the Certifying Authorities;
(i) specifying the terms and conditions subject to which auditors may be appointed and the remuneration to be paid to them;
(j) facilitating the establishment of any electronic system by a Certifying Authority either solely or jointly with other Certifying Authorities and regulation of such systems;
(k) specifying the manner in which the Certifying Authorities shall conduct their dealings with the subscribers;
(l) resolving any conflict of interests between the Certifying Authorities and the subscribers;
(m) laying down the duties of the Certifying Authorities; and
(n) maintaining a data base containing the disclosure record of every Certifying Authority containing such particulars as may be specified by regulations, which shall be accessible to public.

Recognition of foreign Certifying Authorities.—(1) Subject to such conditions and restrictions as may be specified by regulations, the Controller may with the previous approval of the Central Government, and by notification in the Official Gazette, recognise any foreign Certifying Authority as a Certifying Authority for the purposes of this Act.

(2) Where any Certifying Authority is recognised under sub-section (1), the Digital Signature Certificate issued by such Certifying Authority shall be valid for the purposes of this Act.

(3) The Controller may, if he is satisfied that any Certifying Authority has contravened any of the conditions and restrictions subject to which it was granted recognition under sub-section (1) he

may, for reasons to be recorded in writing, by notification in the Official Gazette, revoke such recognition.

20. Controller to act as repository.—(1) The Controller shall be the repository of all Digital Signature Certificates issued under this Act.

(2) The Controller shall—

(a) make use of hardware, software and procedures that are secure from intrusion and misuse; and

(b) observe such other standards as may be prescribed by the Central Government, to ensure that the secrecy and security of the digital signatures are assured.

(3) The Controller shall maintain a computerised data base of all public keys in such a manner that such data base and the public keys are available to any member of the public.

Licence to issue Digital Signature Certificates.—(1) Subject to the provisions of sub-section (2), any person may make an application, to the Controller, for a licence to issue Digital Signature Certificates.

(2) No licence shall be issued under sub-section (1), unless the applicant fulfils such requirements with respect to qualification, expertise, manpower, financial resources and other infrastructure facilities, which are necessary to issue Digital Signature Certificates as may be prescribed by the Central Government

(3) A licence granted under this section shall—

(a) be valid for such period as may be prescribed by the Central Government;

(b) not be transferable or heritable; and

(c) be subject to such terms and conditions as may be specified by the regulations.

Application for licence.—(1) Every application for issue of a licence shall be in such form as may be prescribed by the Central Government.

(2) Every application for issue of a licence shall be accompanied by—

(a) a certification practice statement;

(b) a statement including the procedures with respect to identification of the applicant;

(c) payment of such fees, not exceeding twenty-five thousand rupees as may be prescribed by the Central Government; and

(d) such other documents, as may be prescribed by the Central Government.

Renewal of licence.—An application for renewal of a licence shall be—

(a) in such form; and
(b) accompanied by such fees, not exceeding five thousand rupees,

as may be prescribed by the Central Government and shall be made not less than forty-five days before the date of expiry of the period of validity of the licence.

Procedure for grant or rejection of licence.—The Controller may, on receipt of an application under sub-section (1) of section 21, after considering the documents accompanying the application and such other factors, as he deems fit, grant the licence or reject the application:

Provided that no application shall be rejected under this section unless the applicant has been given a reasonable opportunity of presenting his case.

Suspension of licence.—(1) The Controller may, if he is satisfied after making such inquiry, as he may think fit, that a Certifying Authority has,—

(a) made a statement in, or in relation to, the application for the issue or renewal of the licence, which is incorrect or false in material particulars;
(b) failed to comply with the terms and conditions subject to which the licence was granted;
(c) failed to maintain the standards specified under clause (b) of sub-section (2) of section 20; and
(d) contravened any provisions of this Act, rule, regulation or order made thereunder, revoke the licence:

Provided that no licence shall be revoked unless the Certifying Authority has been given a reasonable opportunity of showing cause against the proposed revocation.

(2) The Controller may, if he has reasonable cause to believe that there is any ground for revoking a licence under sub-section (1), by order suspend such licence pending the completion of any inquiry ordered by him:

Provided that no licence shall be suspended for a period exceeding ten days unless the Certifying Authority has been given a reasonable opportunity of showing cause against the proposed suspension.

(3) No Certifying Authority whose licence has been suspended shall issue any Digital Signature Certificate during such suspension.

Notice of suspension or revocation of licence.—(1) Where the licence of the Certifying Authority is suspended or revoked, the Controller shall publish notice of such suspension or revocation, as the case may be, in the database maintained by him.

(2) Where one or more repositories are specified, the Controller shall publish notices of such suspension or revocation, as the case may be, in all such repositories:

Provided that the data base containing the notice of such suspension or revocation, as the case may be, shall be made available through a web site which shall be accessible round the clock:

Provided further that the Controller may, if he considers necessary, publicise the contents of database in such electronic or other media, as he may consider appropriate.

Power to delegate.—The Controller may, in writing, authorise the Deputy Controller, Assistant Controller or any officer to exercise any of the powers of the Controller under this Chapter.

Power to investigate contraventions.—(1) The Controller or any officer authorised by him in this behalf shall take up for investigation any contravention of the provisions of this Act, rules or regulations made thereunder.

(2) The Controller or any officer authorised by him in this behalf shall exercise the like powers which are conferred on Income-tax authorities under Chapter XIII of the Income-tax Act, 1961 and shall exercise such powers, subject to such limitations laid down under that Act.

Access to computers and data.—(1) Without prejudice to the provisions of sub-section (1) of section 69, the Controller or any person authorised by him shall, if he has reasonable cause to suspect that any contravention of the provisions of this Act, rules or regulations made thereunder has been committed, have access to any computer system, any apparatus, data or any other material connected with such system, for the purpose of searching or causing a search to be made for obtaining any information or data contained in or available to such computer system.

(2) For the purposes of sub-section (1), the Controller or any person authorised by him may, by order, direct any person incharge of, or otherwise concerned with the operation of, the computer system, data apparatus or material, to provide him with such reasonable technical and other assistance as he may consider necessary.

Certifying Authority to follow certain procedures.—Every Certifying Authority shall,—

(a) make use of hardware, software and procedures that are secure from intrusion and misuse;

(b) provide a reasonable level of reliability in its services which are reasonably suited to the performance of intended functions;

(c) adhere to security procedures to ensure that the secrecy and privacy of the digital signatures are assured; and

(d) observe such other standards as may be specified by regulations.

Certifying Authority to ensure compliance of the Act, etc.—Every Certifying Authority shall ensure that every person employed or otherwise engaged by it complies, in the course of his employment or engagement, with the provisions of this Act, rules, regulations and orders made thereunder.

Display of licence.—Every Certifying Authority shall display its licence at a conspicuous place of the premises in which it carries on its business.

33. Surrender of licence.—(1) Every Certifying Authority whose licence is suspended or revoked shall immediately after such suspension or revocation, surrender the licence to the Controller.

(2) Where any Certifying Authority fails to surrender a licence under sub-section (1), the person in whose favour a licence is issued, shall be guilty of an offence and shall be punished with imprisonment which may extend up to six months or a fine which may extend up to ten thousand rupees or with both.

Disclosure.—(1) Every Certifying Authority shall disclose in the manner specified by regulations—

(a) its Digital Signature Certificate which contains the public key corresponding to the private key used by that Certifying Authority to digitally sign another

Digital Signature Certificate;

(b) any certification practice statement relevant thereto;

(c) notice of the revocation or suspension of its Certifying Authority Certificate, if any; and

(d) any other fact that materially and adversely affects either the reliability of a Digital Signature Certificate, which that Authority has issued, or the Authority's ability to perform its services.

(2) Where in the opinion of the Certifying Authority any event has occurred or any situation has arisen which may materially and adversely affect the integrity of its computer system or the conditions subject to which a Digital Signature Certificate was granted, then, the Certifying Authority shall—

(a) use reasonable efforts to notify any person who is likely to be affected by that occurrence; or

(b) act in accordance with the procedure specified in its certification practice statement to deal with such event or situation.

7.8 DIGITAL SIGNATURE CERTIFICATES

Certifying Authority to issue Digital Signature Certificate.—(1) Any person may make an application to the Certifying Authority for the issue of a Digital Signature Certificate in such form as may be prescribed by the Central Government.

(2) Every such application shall be accompanied by such fee not exceeding twenty-five thousand rupees as may be prescribed by the Central Government, to be paid to the Certifying Authority:

Provided that while prescribing fees under sub-section (2) different fees may be prescribed for different classes of applicants.

(3) Every such application shall be accompanied by a certification practice statement or where there is no such statement, a statement containing such particulars, as may be specified by regulations.

(4) On receipt of an application under sub-section (1), the Certifying Authority may, after consideration of the certification practice statement or the other statement under sub-section (3) and after making such enquiries as it may deem fit, grant the Digital Signature Certificate or for reasons to be recorded in writing, reject the application:

Provided that no Digital Signature Certificate shall be granted unless the Certifying Authority is satisfied that—

(a) the applicant holds the private key corresponding to the public key to be listed in the Digital Signature Certificate;

(b) the applicant holds a private key, which is capable of creating a digital signature; and

(c) the public key to be listed in the certificate can be used to verify a digital signature affixed by the private key held by the applicant:

Provided further that no application shall be rejected unless the applicant has been given a reasonable opportunity of showing cause against the proposed rejection.

Representations upon issuance of Digital Signature Certificate.— A Certifying Authority while issuing a Digital Signature Certificate shall certify that—

(a) it has complied with the provisions of this Act and the rules and regulations made thereunder;

(b) it has published the Digital Signature Certificate or otherwise made it available to such person relying on it and the subscriber has accepted it;

(c) the subscriber holds the private key corresponding to the public key, listed in the Digital Signature Certificate;

(d) the subscriber's public key and private key constitute a functioning key pair;

(e) the information contained in the Digital Signature Certificate is accurate; and

(f) it has no knowledge of any material fact, which if it had been included in the Digital Signature Certificate would adversely affect the reliability of the representations made in clauses (a) to (d).

Suspension of Digital Signature Certificate.—(1) Subject to the provisions of sub-section (2), the Certifying Authority which has issued a Digital Signature Certificate may suspend such Digital Signature Certificate,—

(a) on receipt of a request to that effect from—

(i) the subscriber listed in toe Digital Signature Certificate; or

(ii) any person duly authorised to act on behalf of that subscriber,

(b) if it is of opinion that the Digital Signature Certificate should be suspended in public interest.

(2) A Digital Signature Certificate shall not be suspended for a period exceeding fifteen days unless the subscriber has been given an opportunity of being heard in the matter.

(3) On suspension of a Digital Signature Certificate under this section, the Certifying Authority shall communicate the same to the subscriber.

Revocation of Digital Signature Certificate.—(1) A Certifying Authority may revoke a Digital Signature Certificate issued by it—

(a) where the subscriber or any other person authorised by him makes a request to that effect; or

(b) upon the death of the subscriber, or

(c) upon the dissolution of the firm or winding up of the company where the subscriber is a firm or a company.

(2) Subject to the provisions of sub-section (3) and without prejudice to the provisions of sub-section (1), a Certifying Authority may revoke a Digital Signature Certificate which has been issued by it at any time, if it is of opinion that—

(a) a material fact represented in the Digital Signature Certificate is false or has been concealed;

(b) a requirement for issuance of the Digital Signature Certificate was not satisfied;

(c) the Certifying Authority's private key or security system was compromised in a manner materially affecting the Digital Signature Certificate's reliability; and

(d) the subscriber has been declared insolvent or dead or where a subscriber is a firm or a company, which has been dissolved, wound-up or otherwise ceased to exist.

(3) A Digital Signature Certificate shall not be revoked unless the subscriber has been given an opportunity of being heard in the matter.

(4) On revocation of a Digital Signature Certificate under this section, the Certifying Authority shall communicate the same to the subscriber.

7.9 DUTIES OF SUBSCRIBERS

Generating key pair.—Where any Digital Signature Certificate, the public key of which corresponds to the private key of that subscriber which is to be listed in the Digital Signature Certificate has been accepted by a subscriber, then, the subscriber shall generate the key pair by applying the security procedure.

Acceptance of Digital Signature Certificate.—(1) A subscriber shall be deemed to have accepted a Digital Signature Certificate if he publishes or authorises the publication of a Digital Signature Certificate—

(a) to one or more persons; and

(b) in a repository, or otherwise demonstrates his approval of the Digital Signature Certificate in any manner.

(2) By accepting a Digital Signature Certificate the subscriber certifies to all who reasonably rely on the information contained in the Digital Signature Certificate that—

(a) the subscriber holds the private key corresponding to the public key listed in the Digital Signature Certificate and is entitled to hold the same;

(b) all representations made by the subscriber to the Certifying Authority and all material relevant to the information contained in the Digital Signature Certificate are true; and

(c) all information in the Digital Signature Certificate that is within the knowledge of the subscriber is true.

Control of private key.—(1) Every subscriber shall exercise reasonable care to retain control of the private key corresponding to the public key listed in his Digital Signature Certificate and take all steps to prevent its disclosure to a person not authorised to affix the digital signature of the subscriber.

(2) If the private key corresponding to the public key listed in the Digital Signature Certificate has been compromised, then, the subscriber shall communicate the same without any delay to the Certifying Authority in such manner as may be specified by the regulations.

Explanation.—For the removal of doubts, it is hereby declared that the subscriber shall be liable till he has informed the Certifying Authority that the private key has been compromised.

7.10 PENALTIES AND ADJUDICATION

Penalty for damage to computer, computer system, etc.—If any person without permission of the owner or any other person who is incharge of a computer, computer system or computer network,—

(a) accesses or secures access to such computer, computer system or computer network;

(b) downloads, copies or extracts any data, computer data base or information from such computer, computer system or computer network including information or data held or stored in any removable storage medium;

(c) introduces or causes to be introduced any computer contaminant or computer virus into any computer, computer system or computer network;

(d) damages or causes to be damaged any computer, computer system or computer network, data, computer data base or any other programmes residing in such computer, computer system or computer network;

(e) disrupts or causes disruption of any computer, computer system or computer network;

(f) denies or causes the denial of access to any person authorised to access any computer, computer system or computer network by any means;

(g) provides any assistance to any person to facilitate access to a computer, computer system or computer network in contravention of the provisions of this Act, rules or regulations made thereunder;

(h) charges the services availed of by a person to the account of another person by tampering with or manipulating any computer, computer system, or computer network, he shall be liable to pay damages by way of compensation not exceeding one crore rupees to the person so affected.

Explanation.—For the purposes of this section,—

(i) "computer contaminant" means any set of computer instructions that are designed—

  (a) to modify, destroy, record, transmit data or programme residing within a computer, computer system or computer network; or

  (b) by any means to usurp the normal operation of the

computer, computer system, or computer network;

(ii) "computer data base" means a representation of information, knowledge, facts, concepts or instructions in text, image, audio, video that are being prepared or have been prepared in a formalised manner or have been produced by a computer, computer system or computer network and are intended for use in a computer, computer system or computer network;

(iii) "computer virus" means any computer instruction, information, data or programme that destroys, damages, degrades or adversely affects the performance of a computer resource or attaches itself to another computer resource and operates when a programme, data or instruction is executed or some other event takes place in that computer resource; and

(iv) "damage" means to destroy, alter, delete, add, modify or rearrange any computer resource by any means.

Penalty for failure to furnish information return, etc.—If any person who is required under this Act or any rules or regulations made thereunder to—

(a) furnish any document, return or report to the Controller or the Certifying Authority fails to furnish the same, he shall be liable to a penalty not exceeding one lakh and fifty thousand rupees for each such failure;

(b) file any return or furnish any information, books or other documents within the time specified therefor in the regulations fails to file return or furnish the same within the time specified therefor in the regulations, he shall be liable to a penalty not exceeding five thousand rupees for every day during which such failure continues; and

(c) maintain books of account or records, fails to maintain the same, he shall be liable to a penalty not exceeding ten thousand rupees for every day during which the failure continues.

Residuary penalty.—Whoever contravenes any rules or regulations made under this Act, for the contravention of which no penalty has been separately provided, shall be liable to pay a compensation not exceeding twenty-five thousand rupees to the person affected by such contravention or a penalty not exceeding twenty-five thousand rupees.

Power to adjudicate.—(1) For the purpose of adjudging under this Chapter whether any person has committed a contravention of any of the provisions of this Act or of any rule, regulation, direction or order made thereunder the Central Government shall, subject to the provisions of sub-section (3), appoint any officer not below the rank of a Director to the Government of India or an equivalent officer of a State Government to be an adjudicating officer for holding an inquiry in the manner prescribed by the Central Government.

7.11 THE CYBER REGULATIONS APPELLATE TRIBUNAL

Establishment of Cyber Appellate Tribunal.—(1) The Central Government shall, by notification, establish one or more appellate tribunals to be known as the Cyber Regulations Appellate Tribunal.

(2) The Central Government shall also specify, in the notification referred to in sub-section (1), the matters and places in relation to which the Cyber Appellate Tribunal may exercise jurisdiction.

Composition of Cyber Appellate Tribunal.—A Cyber Appellate Tribunal shall consist of one person only (hereinafter referred to as the Residing Officer of the Cyber Appellate Tribunal) to be appointed, by notification, by the Central Government.

7.12 TECHNICAL ASPECTS

Technological advancements have created new possibilities for criminal activity, in particular the criminal misuse of information technologies such as

a. Unauthorized access and Hacking

Access means gaining entry into, instructing or communicating with the logical, arithmetical, or memory function resources of a computer, computer system or computer network.

Unauthorized access would therefore mean any kind of access without the permission of either the rightful owner or the person in charge of a computer, computer system or computer network.

Every act committed towards breaking into a computer and/or network is hacking. Hackers write or use ready-made computer programs to attack the target computer. They possess the desire to destruct and they get the kick out of such destruction. Some hackers hack for personal monetary gains, such as to stealing the credit card information, transferring money from various bank accounts to their own account followed by withdrawal of money.

By hacking web server taking control on another persons website called as web hijacking.

b. Trojan Attack

The program that act like something useful but do the things that are quiet damping. The programs of this kind are called as Trojans.

The name Trojan Horse is popular.

Trojans come in two parts, a Client part and a Server part. When the victim (unknowingly) runs the server on its machine, the attacker will then use the Client to connect to the Server and start using the trojan.

TCP/IP protocol is the usual protocol type used for communications, but some functions of the trojans use the UDP protocol as well.

c. Virus and Worm Attack

A program that has capability to infect other programs and make copies of itself and spread into other programs is called virus.

Programs that multiply like viruses but spread from computer to computer are called as worms.

d. E-mail & IRC related Crimes

1. **Email spoofing:** Email spoofing refers to email that appears to have been originated from one source when it was actually sent from another source. Please Read

2. **Email Spamming:** Email "spamming" refers to sending email to thousands and thousands of users—similar to a chain letter.

3. **Sending malicious codes through email**: E-mails are used to send viruses, Trojans etc through emails as an attachment or by sending a link of website which on visiting downloads malicious code.

4. **Email bombing:** E-mail "bombing" is characterized by abusers repeatedly sending an identical email message to a particular address.

5. **Sending threatening emails**

6. **Defamatory emails**

7. **Email frauds**

8. **IRC related**

Three main ways to attack IRC are: “verbala[?18218;?T#8220; attacks, clone attacks, and flood attacks.”

e. Denial of Service Attacks

Flooding a computer resource with more requests than it can handle. This causes the resource to crash thereby denying access of service to authorized users.

Examples include

- attempts to “flood” a network, thereby preventing legitimate network traffic
- attempts to disrupt connections between two machines, thereby preventing access to a service
- attempts to prevent a particular individual from accessing a service
- attempts to disrupt service to a specific system or person.

7.13 OFFENCES

Hacking with computer system.—(1) Whoever with the intent to cause or knowing that he is likely to cause wrongful loss or damage to the public or any person destroys or deletes or alters any information residing in a computer resource or diminishes its value or utility or affects it injuriously by any means, commits hack:

(2) Whoever commits hacking shall be punished with imprisonment up to three years, or with fine which may extend upto two lakh rupees, or with both.

Publishing of information which is obscene in electronic form.—Whoever publishes or transmits or causes to be published in the electronic form, any material which is lascivious or appeals to the prurient interest or if its effect is such as to tend to deprave and corrupt persons who are likely, having regard to all relevant circumstances, to read, see or hear the matter contained or embodied in it, shall be punished on first conviction with imprisonment of either description for a term which may extend to five years and with fine which may extend to one lakh rupees and in the event of a second or subsequent conviction with imprisonment of either description for a term which may extend to ten years and also with fine which may extend to two lakh rupees.

7.14 PREVENTION OF FRAUD

Introduction

The world's population is large, people are busy, and the processes of society are complex. To date, no society has been able to prevent all criminal acts, and few have been silly enough to even set out to do so. In a free society, law enforcement agencies are significantly limited in the extent to which they can exercise powers and tools to prevent crime. The relative success of crime prevention has varied widely, and appears to depend on a balance between 'carrot' and 'stick' mechanisms appropriate to each particular culture.

New technologies are being applied to crime prevention, such as video-surveillance and data surveillance .

In the context of the Internet, several approaches can be applied in an attempt to prevent criminal activity:

'hard' prevention, in the sense of intrisic features within the architecture, protocols and software, that preclude, or render difficult, actions of a criminal nature from being performed;

'soft' prevention, comprising disincentives against criminal activity, and in particular:

- clear definition of criminal offences;
- public awareness-raising and education;
- the perceived likelihood of discovery;
- the perceived likelihood of effective investigation; and
- the perceived likelihood of successful prosecution.

'Hard' Prevention: 'Hard' prevention is an attractive idea. Unfortunately, it is largely infeasible. This is because most criminal activities are only differentiable from non-criminal ones on the basis of the content or purpose of transmitted data, and hence little scope exists for designing Internet architecture or protocols in order to ensure that the Internet simply cannot be used for criminal purposes.

Some exceptions need to be considered, particularly in relation to—

The transfer of value: There is a need for architecture, protocols and software that resist misuse.

Internet-connected devices that act on their environment (i.e. are robotic in nature—see Clarke 1993). There is a need for architecture, protocols and software that preclude accidental and trivially simple intentional manipulation by inappropriate users, and in inappropriate ways; and **anonymous and pseudonymous transactions.** There is a need for architecture, protocols and software that implement an appropriate balance between the often conflicting interests of privacy and of accountability.

'Soft' Prevention—Definition, Awareness and Education: Awareness of the existence of a criminal offence, and education as to what it entails, can only be successful if the message is clear. Hence it is fundamental to the prevention of crime that members of the public understand what the activities are that are proscribed, and where the boundaries lie. Many 'white-collar' crimes (such as 'insider trading') suffer in this regard, as do so-called "computer crimes'. A further need is that the definition of criminal offences, and the punishment meted out to miscreants, reflects public opinion.

'Soft' Prevention—The Likelihood of Sanctions: The likelihood of successful prosecution depends on many factors, most of which are not fundamentally changed by the advent of the Internet. Two major new considerations, however, are the questions of:

Jurisdiction: The greatly increased scope for criminal activity to go trans-jurisdictional, extra-jurisdictional and supra-jurisdictional is discussed in Clarke (1997a) and Clarke (1997c), and is not further considered here; and

Forensics: New challenges arise in relation to the collection and presentation of evidentiary trails that satisfy the courts and are difficult to rebut.

Conclusion

1. IT Act, 2008 was developed to promote the IT industry, regulate e-commerce, facilitate e-governance and prevent cybercrime.
2. Central Government appoint a Controller of Certifying Authorities for the purposes of this Act.
3. Controller supervise and specify the conditions subject to which the Certifying authorities shall conduct their business.
4. Central government establish one or more tribunals to be known as the Cyber Regulation Appellate Tribunal.
5. Certifying Authority to issue Digital Signature Certificate to any person as prescribed by Central Government. But it can be revoked if the person authorized makes a request to that effect or upon the

death of subscriber or on dissolution of firm.

6. There is penalty for damage to computer, computer system and for failure to furnish information return etc.
7. Technological advancements have created new possibilities for criminal activity, in particular the criminal misuse of information technologies such as hacking, Trojan attack and virus etc.
8. In the context of the Internet, several approaches can be applied in an attempt to prevent criminal activity such as hard prevention and soft prevention.

TEST QUESTIONS

1. Describe the objectives and scope of the Information Technology Act, 2000.
2. Name the instruments or documents to which IT Act is not applicable.
3. Define the following terms under the Act:
   (a) Appropriate government
   (b) Computer
   (c) Computer system
   (d) Data
   (e) Digital signature
   (f) Electronic record
   (g) Key pair
4. Who may authenticate an electronic record? How is it effected?
5. Describe the provisions of the Act relating to attribution, acknowledgement and dispatch of electronic records.
6. Explain the provisions regarding secure electronic records and secure digital signature.
7. How the controller of certifying authorties is appointed? Discuss the function of the controller.
8. Who can grant a license to issue Digital Signature Certificates ? Explain the various formalties involved in it.
9. Explain the duties of the Certifying Authority and Subscriber.

8

Consumer Protection Act, 1986

LEARNING OBJECTIVES

8.1 Introduction
8.2 Consumer Protection Act, 1986
8.3 Consumer Rights
8.4 Definitions
8.5 Consumer Protection Councils
8.6 Consumer Disputes Redressal Agencies
8.7 Composition of the District Forum
8.8 Composition of the State Commission
8.9 Composition of the National Commission
8.10 Appeal
8.11 Penalties
8.12 Miscellaneous
8.13 Conclusion

8.1 INTRODUCTION

In today's globalised market under open competition it is clear that consumer is a king pin the market. The producer should produce goods keeping in mind the requirements of consumers and satisfy the consumer but it is observed that this obligation is neglected by some businessmen and they are involved is the unfair practice such as supply of quality, adulteration, etc. A common consumer is not in a position to fight for his rights on his own unless and until a legal and organized help is provided to consumers. In this direction, central government took a very big initiative by establishing Consumer Protection Act in 1986.

Need for Consumer Protection

1. **Poverty and Unemployment:** In the developing country most of the customers are poor and unemployed. They accept anything which is offer to them at low price. The poor consumers are the most harassed and the most helpless creature in India.
2. **Illiterate Consumer**: In developing countries like India most of the consumers are uneducated and illiterate. They cannot differentiate between the pure and adulterated product. Consumer cannot read the contents, date, price, quantity, etc. So they really blindly on the information of the suppliers.
3. **Consumers are not organised**: Another reason for more requirement of consumer protection in India is that in India consumers have not yet organised themselves to have powerful consumer movement. They are lack of effective agencies to secure redressal of their grievances.

8.2 CONSUMER PROTECTION ACT, 1986

Enactment of Consumer Protection Act, 1986 was one of the most important steps taken to protect the interest of consumer. The provision of act came into force from July 1, 1987. The main features of this Act are:

1. This act has provide various right and responsibilities to consumers.
2. It provides safeguard to consumers against the defective goods, deficients, services, and other from theory of exploitation.

8.3 CONSUMER RIGHTS

Although businessman is aware of his social responsibilities even then we come across many cases of consumer exploitation. That why government of India provided following rights to all the consumers under the consumer protection act:

1. **Right to safety:** According to this right the consumers have

right to be protected against the marketing of goods and services which are hazardous to life and property. This right is important for safe and secure life.

2. **Right to information**: According to this right the consumer has right to get information about the quality, quantity, purity standard and piece of goods or Services. The producer must supply all the relevant information at a suitable place.
3. **Right to choice**: According to this right very consumer has right to choose the goods or services of his or her likings. The suppliers should not force the customer to buy a particular brand only. Consumer should be free to choose the most suitable product from his point of view.
4. **Right to consumer education**: According to this right it is the right of consumer to acquire knowledge and skill to be informed to customer. It is easier for literate consumers to know their rights and take actions.
5. **Right to seek redressal**: According to this right the consumer has the right get compensation or seek redressal against unfair trade practices or any other exploitation. This right assures justice to consumer against exploitation.
6. **Right to heard/Right to representation**: According to this right the consumer has the right to represent himself or to be heard or right to advocate his interest. In case a consumer has been exploited or has any complaint against the product or service then he has the right to be heard.

Short title, extent, commencement and application

(1) This Act may be called the Consumer Protection Act, 1986. (2) It extends to the whole of India except the State of Jammu and Kashmir. (3) It shall come into force on such date as the Central Government may, by notification, appoint and different dates may be appointed for different States and for different provisions of this Act. (4) Save as otherwise expressly provided by the Central Government by notification, this Act shall apply to all goods and services.

8.4 DEFINITIONS

1. **Appropriate laboratory:** "Appropriate laboratory" means a laboratory or organization recognised by the Central Government or

by a State Government, subject to such guidelines as may be prescribed by the Central Government in this behalf; any such laboratory or organisation established by or under any law for the time being in force, which is maintained, financed or aided by the Central Government or a State Government for carrying out analysis or test of any goods with a view to determining whether such goods suffer from any defect.

2. **Branch Office:** "Branch office" means—
   I. any establishment described as a branch by the opposite party; or
   II. any establishment carrying on either the same or substantially the same activity as that carried on by the head office of the establishment;
3. **Complainant:** "Complainant" means—
   I. a consumer; or
   II. any voluntary consumer association registered under the Companies Act, 1956 (1 of 1956) or under any other law for the time being in force; or
   III. the Central Government or any State Government; or
   IV. one or more consumers, where there are numerous consumers having the same interest; and
   V. in case of death of a consumer, his legal heir or representative; who or which makes a complaint.

4. **Complaint:** "Complaint" means any allegation in writing made by a complainant that—
   I. an unfair trade practice or a restrictive trade practice has been adopted by any trader or service provider;
   II. the goods bought by him or agreed to be bought by him; suffer from one or more defects;
   III. the services hired or availed of or agreed to be hired or availed of by him suffer from deficiency in any respect;
   IV. a trader or service provider, as the case may be, has charged for the goods or for the service mentioned in the complaint a price in excess of the price—
      (a) fixed by or under any law for the time being in force;
      (b) displayed on the goods or any package containing such goods ;
      (c) displayed on the price list exhibited by him by or under

any law for the time being in force; and

(d) agreed between the parties;

V. goods which will be hazardous to life and safety when used or being offered for sale to the public,—

A. in contravention of any standards relating to safety of such goods as required to be complied with, by or under any law for the time being in force; and

B. if the trader could have known with due diligence that the goods so offered are unsafe to the public;

VI. services which are hazardous or likely to be hazardous to life and safety of the public when used, are being offered by the service provider which such person could have known with due diligence to be injurious to life and safety;"

5. **Consumer:** "Consumer" means any person who—

a. buys any goods for a consideration which has been paid or promised or partly paid and partly promised, or under any system of deferred payment and includes any user of such goods other than the person who buys such goods for consideration paid or promised or partly paid or partly promised, or under any system of deferred payment when such use is made with the approval of such person, but does not include a person who obtains such goods for resale or for any commercial purpose; or

b. hires or avails of any services for a consideration which has been paid or promised or partly paid and partly promised, or under any system of deferred payment and includes any beneficiary of such services other than the person who 'hires or avails of the services for consideration paid or promised, or partly paid and partly promised, or under any system of deferred payment, when such services are availed of with the approval of the first mentioned person but does not include a person who avails of such services for any commercial purposes;

Explanation.—For the purposes of this clause, "commercial purpose" does not include use by a person of goods bought and used by him and services availed by him exclusively for the purposes of earning his livelihood by means of self-employment;

6. Consumer Dispute: "Consumer dispute" means a dispute where the person against whom a complaint has been made, denies or disputes the allegations contained in the complaint;

7. Defect: "Defect" means any fault, imperfection or shortcoming in the quality, quantity, potency, purity or standard which is required to be maintained by or under any law for the time being in force under any contract, express or implied or as is claimed by the trader in any manner whatsoever in relation to any goods;

8. Deficiency: "Deficiency" means any fault, imperfection, shortcoming or inadequacy in the quality, nature and manner of performance which is required to be maintained by or under any law for the time being in force or has been undertaken to be performed by a person in pursuance of a contract or otherwise in relation to any service;

9. District Forum: "District Forum" means a Consumer Disputes Redressal Forum established under clause (a) of section 9;

10. Goods: "Goods" means goods as defined in the Sale of Goods Act, 1930 (3 of 1930);

11. Manufacturer: "Manufacturer" means a person who—

a. makes or manufactures any goods or part thereof; or
b. does not make or manufacture any goods but assembles parts thereof made or manufactured by others; or
c. puts or causes to be put his own mark on any goods made or manufactured by any other manufacturer;

Explanation.—Where a manufacturer dispatches any goods or part thereof to any branch office maintained by him, such branch office shall not be deemed to be the manufacturer even though the parts so dispatched to it are assembled at such branch office and are sold or distributed from such branch office;

12. Members: "Member" includes the President and a member of the National Commission or a State Commission or a District Forum, as the case may be;

13. National Commission: "National Commission" means the National Consumer Disputes Redressal Commission established under clause (c) of section 9;

14. Notification: "Notification" means a notification published in the Official Gazette;

15. Person: "Person" includes,—

a. a firm whether registered or not;
b. a Hindu undivided family;
c. a co-operative society; and
d. every other association of persons whether registered under the Societies Registration Act, 1860 (21 of 1860) or not;

16. Prescribed: "Prescribed" means prescribed by rules made by the State Government, or as the case may be, by the Central Government under this Act;

17. Regulation: "Regulation" means the regulations made by the National Commission under this Act;

18. Restrictive Trade Practices: "Restrictive trade practice" means a trade practice which tends to bring about manipulation of price or conditions of delivery or to affect flow of supplies in the market relating to goods or services in such a manner as to impose on the consumers unjustified costs or restrictions and shall include—

(a) delay beyond the period agreed to by a trader in supply of such goods or in providing the services which has led or is likely to lead to rise in the price;
(b) any trade practice which requires a consumer to buy, hire or avail of any goods or, as the case may be, services as condition precedent to buying, hiring or availing of other goods or services;

19. Service: "Service" means service of any description which is made available to potential users and includes, but not limited to, the provision of facilities in connection with banking, financing insurance, transport, processing, supply of electrical or other energy, board or lodging or both, housing construction, entertainment, amusement or the purveying of news or other information, but does not include the rendering of any service free of charge or under a contract of personal service;

20. Spurious goods and services: "Spurious goods and services" mean such goods and services which are claimed to be genuine but they are actually not so;

21. State Commission: "State Commission" means a Consumer Disputes Redressal Commission established in a State under clause (b) of section 9;

22. Trader: "Trader" in relation to any goods means a person who sells or distributes any goods for sale and includes the manufacturer thereof, and where such goods are sold or distributed in package form, includes the packer thereof;

23. Unfair Trade Practices: "Unfair trade practice" means a trade practice which, for the purpose of promoting the sale, use or supply of any goods or for the provision of any service, adopts any unfair method or unfair or deceptive practice including any of the following practices, namely:—

(a) the practice of making any statement, whether orally or in writing or by visible representation which,—

(ii) falsely represents that the goods are of a particular standard, quality, quantity, grade, composition, style or model;

(iii) falsely represents that the services are of a particular standard, quality or grade;

(iv) falsely represents any re-built, second-hand, renovated, reconditioned or old goods as new goods;

(v) represents that the goods or services have sponsorship, approval, performance, characteristics, accessories, uses or benefits which such goods or services do not have;

(vi) represents that the seller or the supplier has a sponsorship or approval or affiliation which such seller or supplier does not have;

(vii) makes a false or misleading representation concerning the need for, or the usefulness of, any goods or services;

(viii) gives to the public any warranty or guarantee of the performance, efficacy or length of life of a product or of any goods that is not based on an adequate or proper test thereof;

(b) Provided that where a defence is raised to the effect that such warranty or guarantee is based on adequate or proper test, the burden of proof of such defence shall lie on the person raising such defence;

(c) (viii) makes to the public a representation in a form that purports to be—

(i) a warranty or guarantee of a product or of any goods or services;

(ii) a promise to replace, maintain or repair an article or any part thereof or to repeat or continue a service until it has achieved a specified result, if such purported warranty or guarantee or promise is materially misleading or if there is no reasonable prospect that such warranty, guarantee or promise will be carried out;

(iii) materially misleads the public concerning the price at which a product or like products or goods or services, have been or are, ordinarily sold or provided, and, for this purpose, a representation as to price shall be deemed to refer to the price at which the product or goods or services has or have been sold by sellers or provided by suppliers generally in the relevant market unless it is clearly specified to be the price at which the product has been sold or services have been provided by the person by whom or on whose behalf the representation is made;

(iv) gives false or misleading facts disparaging the goods, services or trade of another person.

Explanation.—For the purposes of clause (1), a statement that is—

(a) expressed on an article offered or displayed for sale, or on its wrapper or container; or

(b) expressed on anything attached to, inserted in, or accompanying, an article offered or displayed for sale, or on anything on which the article is mounted for display or sale; or

(c) contained in or on anything that is sold, sent, delivered, transmitted or in any other manner whatsoever made available to a member of the public; or

(d) shall be deemed to be a statement made to the public by, and only by, the person who had caused the statement to be so expressed, made or contained;

(a) permits the publication of any advertisement whether in any newspaper or otherwise, for the sale or supply at a bargain price, of goods or services that are not intended to be offered for sale or supply at the bargain price, or for a period that is, and in quantities that are, reasonable, having regard to the nature of the market in which the business is carried on, the nature and size of business, and the nature of the advertisement.

Explanation.—For the purpose of clause (2), "bargaining price" means—

(b) a price that is stated in any advertisement to be a bargain price, by reference to an ordinary price or otherwise, or

(c) a price that a person who reads, hears or sees the advertisement, would reasonably understand to be a bargain price having regard to the prices at which the product advertised or like products are ordinarily sold;

(d) permits—

1. the offering of gifts, prizes or other items with the intention of not providing them as offered or creating impression that something is being given or offered free of charge when it is fully or partly covered by the amount charged in the transaction as a whole;
2. the conduct of any contest, lottery, game of chance or skill, for the purpose of promoting, directly or indirectly, the sale, use or supply of any product or any business interest;

(e) (3A) withholding from the participants of any scheme offering gifts, prizes or other items free of charge, on its closure the information about final results of the scheme.

Explanation.—For the purposes of this sub-clause, the participants of a scheme shall be deemed to have been informed of the final results of the scheme where such results are within a reasonable time, published, prominently in the same newspapers in which the scheme was originally advertised;

(a) permits the sale or supply of goods intended to be used, or are of a kind likely to be used, by consumers, knowing or having reason to believe that the goods do not comply with the standards prescribed by competent authority relating to performance, composition, contents, design, constructions, finishing or packaging as are necessary to prevent or reduce the risk of injury to the person using the goods;

(b) permits the hoarding or destruction of goods, or refuses to sell the goods or to make them available for sale or to provide any service, if such hoarding or destruction or refusal raises or tends to raise or is intended to raise, the cost of those or other similar goods or services.

(c) manufacture of spurious goods or offering such goods for sale or adopts deceptive practices in the provision of services.

(f) (2) Any reference in this Act to any other Act or provision thereof which is not in force in any area to which this Act applies shall be construed to have a reference to the corresponding Act or provision thereof in force in such area.

(g) Act not in derogation of any other law.—The provisions of this Act shall be in addition to and not in derogation of the provisions of any other law for the time being in force.

8.5 CONSUMER PROTECTION COUNCILS

Consumer protection councils are established to promote and protect the interests of the consumers. These councils are advisory bodies and established in three-tier structure at Central, state and district level.

Establishment of Central Consumer Protection Council: The Central Consumer Protection Council.—(1) The Central Government shall, by notification, establish with effect from such date as it may specify in such notification, a Council to be known as the Central Consumer Protection Council (hereinafter referred to as the Central Council).

(2) The Central Council shall consist of the following members, namely:—

(a) the Minister-in-charge of the consumer affairs in the Central Government, who shall be its Chairman, and

(b) such number of other official or non-official members representing such interests as may be prescribed.

Procedure for meetings of the Central Council.—(1) The Central Council shall meet as and when necessary, but at least one meeting of the Council shall be held every year.

(2) The Central Council shall meet at such time and place as the Chairman may think fit and shall observe such procedure in regard to the transaction of its business as may be prescribed.

Objects of the Central Council.—The objects of the Central Council shall be to promote and protect the rights of the consumers such as,—

(a) the right to be protected against the marketing of goods and services which are hazardous to life and property;
(b) the right to be informed about the quality, quantity, potency, purity, standard and price of goods or services, as the case may be so as to protect the consumer against unfair trade practices;
(c) the right to be assured, wherever possible, access to a variety of goods and services at competitive prices;
(d) the right to be heard and to be assured that consumer's interests will receive due consideration at appropriate forums;
(e) the right to seek redressal against unfair trade practices or restrictive trade practices or unscrupulous exploitation of consumers; and
(f) the right to consumer education.

Establishment of State Consumer Protection Council.—The State Government shall, by notification, establish with effect from such date as it may specify in such notification, a Council to be known as the Consumer Protection Council for................... (hereinafter referred to as the State Council), shall consist of the following members, namely:—

(a) the Minister-in-charge of consumer affairs in the State Government who shall be its Chairman;
(b) such number of other official or non-official members representing such interests as may be prescribed by the State Government;

(c) such number of other official or non-official members, not exceeding ten, as may be nominated by the Central Government.

(3) The State Council shall meet as and when necessary but not less than two meetings shall be held every year.

(4) The State Council shall meet at such time and place as the Chairman may think fit and shall observe such procedure in regard to the transaction of its business as may be prescribed by the State Government.

Objects of the State Council.—The objects of every State Council shall be to promote and protect within the State the rights of the consumers laid down in clauses (a) to (f) of section 6.

District Consumer Protection Council.—The State Government shall establish for every district, by notification, a council to be known as the District Consumer Protection Council with effect from such date as it may specify in such notification.

The District Consumer Protection Council (hereinafter referred to as the District Council) shall consist of the following members, namely:—

(a) the Collector of the district (by whatever name called), who shall be its Chairman; and

(b) such number of other official and non-official members representing such interests as may be prescribed by the State Government.

(3) The District Council shall meet as and when necessary but not less than two meetings shall be held every year.

(4) The District Council shall meet at such time and place within the district as the Chairman may think fit and shall observe such procedure in regard to the transaction of its business as may be prescribed by the State Government.

Objects of District Consumer Protection Council—The objects of every District Council shall be to promote and protect within the district the rights of the consumers laid down in clauses (a) to (f) of section 6.

8.6 CONSUMER DISPUTES REDRESSAL AGENCIES

Establishment of Consumer Disputes Redressal Agencies.—There shall be established for the purposes of this Act, the following agencies, namely:—

(a) a Consumer Disputes Redressal Forum to be known as the "District Forum" established by the State Government in each district of the State by notification:
Provided that the State Government may, if it deems fit, establish more than one District Forum in a district.

(b) a Consumer Disputes Redressal Commission to be known as the "State Commission" established by the State Government in the State by notification; and

(c) a National Consumer Disputes Redressal Commission established by the Central Government by notification.

8.7 COMPOSITION OF THE DISTRICT FORUM

Composition of the District Forum.—(1) Each District Forum shall consist of,—

(a) a person who is, or has been, or is qualified to be a District Judge, who shall be its President;

(b) two other members, one of whom shall be a woman, who shall have the following qualifications, namely:—

I. be not less than thirty-five years of age,

II. possess a bachelor's degree from a recognised university,

III. be persons of ability, integrity and standing, and have adequate knowledge and experience of at least ten years in dealing with problems relating to economics, law, commerce, accountancy, industry, public affairs or administration:

Provided that a person shall be disqualified for appointment as a member if he—

(a) has been convicted and sentenced to imprisonment for an offence which, in the opinion of the state Government involves moral turpitude; or

(b) is an undischarged insolvent; or

(c) is of unsound mind and stands so declared by a competent court; or

(d) has been removed or dismissed from the service of the Government or a body corporate owned or controlled by the Government; or

(e) has, in the opinion of the state Government, such

financial or other interest as is likely to affect prejudicially the discharge by him of his functions as a member; or

(f) has such other disqualifications as may be prescribed by the State Government;

Every appointment under sub-section (I) shall be made by the State Government on the recommendation of a selection committee consisting of the following, namely:—

(i) the President of the State Commission—Chairman.
(ii) Secretary, Law Department of the State—Member.
(iii) Secretary incharge of the Department dealing with consumer affairs in the State—Member.

Provided that where the President of the State Commission is, by reason of absence or otherwise, unable to act as Chairman of the Selection Committee, the State Government may refer the matter to the Chief Justice of the High Court for nominating a sitting Judge of that High Court to act as Chairman.

(2) Every member of the District Forum shall hold office for a term of five years or up to the age of sixty-five years, whichever is earlier:

Provided that a member shall be eligible for re-appointment for another term of five years or up to the age of sixty-five years, whichever is earlier, subject to the condition that he fulfils the qualifications and other conditions for appointment mentioned in clause (b) of sub-section (1) and such re-appointment is also made on the basis of the recommendation of the Selection Committee:

Provided further that a member may resign his office in writing under his hand addressed to the State Government and on such resignation being accepted, his office shall become vacant and may be filled by appointment of a person possessing any of the qualifications mentioned in sub-section (1) in relation to the category of the member who is required to be appointed under the provisions of sub-section (1A) in place of the person who has resigned:

Provided also that a person appointed as the President or as a member, before the commencement of the Consumer Protection (Amendment) Act, 2002, shall continue to hold such office as President or member, as the case may be, till the completion of his term.

(3) The salary or honorarium and other allowances payable to, and the other terms and conditions of service of the members of the District Forum shall be such as may be prescribed by the State Government:

Provided that the appointment of a member on whole-time basis shall be made by the State Government on the recommendation of the President of the State Commission taking into consideration such factors as may be prescribed including the work load of the District Forum.

Jurisdiction of the District Forum.—(1) Subject to the other provisions of this Act, the District Forum shall have jurisdiction to entertain complaints where the value of the goods or services and the compensation, if any, claimed does not exceed rupees twenty lakhs.

(2) A complaint shall be instituted in a District Forum within the local limits of whose jurisdiction,—

(a) the opposite party or each of the opposite parties, where there are more than one, at the time of the institution of the complaint, actually and voluntarily resides or carries on business or has a branch office or personally works for gain, or

(b) any of the opposite parties, where there are more than one, at the time of the institution of the complaint, actually and voluntarily resides, or carries on business or has a branch office, or personally works for gain, provided that in such case either the permission of the District Forum is given, or the opposite parties who do not reside, or carry on business or have a branch office, or personally work for gain, as the case may be, acquiesce in such institution; or

(c) the cause of action, wholly or in part, arises.

Manner in which complaint shall be made.—(1) A complaint in relation to any goods sold or delivered or agreed to be sold or delivered or any service provided or agreed to be provided may be filed with a District Forum by—

(a) the consumer to whom such goods are sold or delivered or agreed to be sold or delivered or such service provided or agreed to be provided;

(b) any recognised consumer association whether the consumer to whom the goods sold or delivered or agreed to be sold or delivered or service provided or agreed to be provided is a member of such association or not;

(c) one or more consumers, where there are numerous consumers having the same interest, with the permission of the District Forum, on behalf of, or for the benefit of, all consumers so interested; or

(d) the Central Government or the State Government, as the case may be, either in its individual capacity or as a representative of interests of the consumers in general.

(2) Every complaint filed under sub-section (1) shall be accompanied with such amount of fee and payable in such manner as may be prescribed.

(3) On receipt of a complaint made under sub-section (1), the District Forum may, by order, allow the complaint to be proceeded with or rejected:

Provided that a complaint shall not be rejected under this section unless an opportunity of being heard has been given to the complainant:

Provided further that the admissibility of the complaint shall ordinarily be decided within twenty-one days from the date on which the complaint was received.

(4) Where a complaint is allowed to be proceeded with under sub-section (3), the District Forum may proceed with the complaint in the manner provided under this Act:

Provided that where a complaint has been admitted by the District Forum, it shall not be transferred to any other court or tribunal or any authority set-up by or under any other law for the time being in force.

Explanation.—For the purpose of this section "recognised consumer association" means any voluntary consumer association registered under the Companies Act, 1956 or any other law for the time being in force".

For the purposes of this section, the District Forum shall have the same powers as are vested in a civil court under Code of Civil Procedure, 1908 while trying a suit in respect of the following matters, namely:—

(i) the summoning and enforcing the attendance of any defendant or witness and examining the witness on oath;

(ii) the discovery and production of any document or other material object producible as evidence;
(iii) the reception of evidence on affidavits;
(iv) the requisitioning of the report of the concerned analysis or test from the appropriate laboratory or from any other relevant source;
(v) issuing of any commission for the examination of any witness, and
(vi) any other matter which may be prescribed.

(5) Every proceeding before the District Forum shall be deemed to be a judicial proceeding within the meaning of sections 193 and 228 of the Indian Code (45 of 1860), and the District Forum shall be deemed to be a civil court for the purposes of section 195, and Chapter XXVI of the Code of Criminal Procedure, 1973 (2 of 1974).

(6) Where the complainant is a consumer referred to in sub-clause (iv) of clause (b) of sub-section (1) of section 2, the provisions of rule 8 of Order I of the First Schedule to the Code of Civil Procedure, 1908 (5 of 1908) shall apply subject to the modification that every reference therein to a suit or decree shall be construed as a reference to a complaint or the order of the District Forum thereon.

(7) In the event of death of a complainant who is a consumer or of the opposite party against whom the complaint has been filed, the provisions of Order XXII of the First Schedule to the Code of Civil Procedure, 1908 (5 of 1908) shall apply subject to the modification that every reference therein to the plaintiff and the defendant shall be construed as reference to a complainant or the opposite party, as the case may be.

Finding of the District Forum.—(1) If, after the proceeding conducted under section 13, the District Forum is satisfied that the goods complained against suffer from any of the defects specified in the complaint or that any of the allegations contained in the complaint about the services are proved, it shall issue an order to the opposite party directing him to do one or more of the following things, namely:—

(a) to remove the defect pointed out by the appropriate laboratory from the goods in question;
(b) to replace the goods with new goods of similar description which shall be free from any defect;

(c) to return to the complainant the price, or, as the case may be, the charges paid by the complainant;

(d) to pay such amount as may be awarded by it as compensation to the consumer for any loss or injury suffered by the consumer due to the negligence of the opposite party:
Provided that the District Forum shall have the power to grant punitive damages in such circumstances as it deems fit;

(e) to remove the defects in goods or deficiencies in the services in question;

(f) to discontinue the unfair trade practice or the restrictive trade practice or not to repeat it;

(g) not to offer the hazardous goods for sale;

(h) to withdraw the hazardous goods from being offered for sale;

(ha) to cease manufacture of hazardous goods and to desist from offering services which are hazardous in nature;

(hb) to pay such sum as may be determined by it if it is of the opinion that loss or injury has been suffered by a large number of consumers who are not identifiable conveniently:
Provided that the minimum amount of sum so payable shall not be less than five per cent of the value of such defective goods sold or service provided, as the case may be, to such consumers:
Provided further that the amount so obtained shall be credited in favour of such person and utilized in such manner as may be prescribed;

(hc) to issue corrective advertisement to neutralize the effect of misleading advertisement at the cost of the opposite party responsible for issuing such misleading advertisement;

(i) to provide for adequate costs to parties.

(2) Every proceeding referred to in sub-section (1) shall be conducted by the President of the District Forum and at least one member thereof sitting together:

Provided that where a member, for any reason, is unable to conduct a proceeding till it is completed, the President and the other member shall continue the proceeding from the stage at which it was last heard by the previous member.

(2A) Every order made by the District Forum under sub-section (1) shall be signed by its President and the member or members who conducted the proceeding:

Provided that where the proceeding is conducted by the President and one member and they differ on any point or points, they shall state the point or points on which they differ and refer the same to the other member for hearing on such point or points and the opinion of the majority shall be the order of the District Forum.

(3) Subject to the foregoing provisions, the procedure relating to the conduct of the meetings of the District Forum, its sittings and other matters shall be such as may be prescribed by the State Government.

8.8 COMPOSITION OF THE STATE COMMISSION

Composition of the State Commission: (1) Each State Commission shall consist of—

(a) a person who is or has been a Judge of a High Court, appointed by the State Government, who shall be its President:

Provided that no appointment under this clause shall be made except after consultation with the Chief Justice of the High Court;

(b) not less than two, and not more than such number of members, as may be prescribed, and one of whom shall be a woman, who shall have the following qualifications, namely:—

I. be not less than thirty-five years of age;

II. possess a bachelor's degree from a recognised university; and

III. be persons of ability, integrity and standing, and have adequate knowledge and experience of at least ten years in dealing with problems relating to economics, law, commerce, accountancy, industry, public affairs or administration:

Provided that not more than fifty per cent of the members shall be from amongst persons having a judicial background.

Explanation.—For the purposes of this clause, the expression "persons having judicial background" shall mean persons having knowledge and experience for at least a period of ten years as a presiding officer at the district level court or any tribunal at equivalent level:

Provided further that a person shall be disqualified for appointment as a member if he—

(a) has been convicted and sentenced to imprisonment for an offence which, in the opinion of the State Government, involves moral turpitude; or
(b) is an undischarged insolvent; or
(c) is of unsound mind and stands so declared by a competent court; or
(d) has been removed or dismissed from the service of the Government or a body corporate owned or controlled by the Government; or
(e) has, in the opinion of the State Government, such financial or other interest, as is likely to affect prejudicially the discharge by him of his functions as a member; or
(f) has such other disqualifications as may be prescribed by the State Government.

(1A) Every appointment under sub-section (1) shall be made by the State Government on the recommendation of a Selection Committee consisting of the following members, namely:—

(i) President of the State Commission—Chairman;
(ii) Secretary of the Law Department of the State—Member;
(iii) Secretary incharge of the Department dealing with Consumer Affairs in the State—Member:

Provided that where the President of the State Commission is, by reason of absence or otherwise, unable to act as Chairman of the Selection Committee, the State Government may refer the matter to the Chief Justice of the High Court for nominating a sitting Judge of that High Court to act as Chairman.

(1B) (i) The jurisdiction, powers and authority of the State Commission may be exercised by Benches thereof.

(ii) A Bench may be constituted by the President with one or more members as the President may deem fit.

(iii) If the members of a Bench differ in opinion on any point, the points shall be decided according to the opinion of the majority, if there is a majority, but if the Members are equally divided, they shall state the point or points on which they differ, and make a reference to the President who shall either hear the point or points himself or refer the case for hearing on such point or points by one or more or the other members and such point or points shall be decided according to the opinion of the majority of the members who have heard the case, including those who first heard it.

(2) The salary or honorarium and other allowances payable to, and the other terms and conditions of service of, the members of the State Commission shall be such as may be prescribed by the State Government.

Provided that the appointment of a member on whole-time basis shall be made by the State Government on the recommendation of the President of the State Commission taking into consideration such factors as may be prescribed including the work load of the State Commission.

(3) Every member of the State Commission shall hold office for a term of five years or up to the age of sixty-seven years, whichever is earlier:

Provided that a member shall be eligible for re-appointment for another term of five years or up to the age of sixty-seven years, whichever is earlier, subject to the condition that he fulfils the qualifications and other conditions for appointment mentioned in clause (b) of sub-section (1) and such re-appointment is made on the basis of the recommendation of the Selection Committee:

Provided further that a person appointed as a President of the State Commission shall also be eligible for re-appointment in the manner provided in clause (a) of sub-section (1) of this section:

Provided also that a member may resign his office in writing under his hand addressed to the State Government and on such resignation being accepted, his office shall become vacant and may be filled by appointment of a person possessing any of the qualifications mentioned in sub-section (1) in relation to the category of the member who is required to be appointed under the provisions of sub-section (1A) in place of the person who has resigned.

(4) Notwithstanding anything contained in sub-section (3), a person appointed as the President or as a member, before the commencement of the Consumer Protection (Amendment) Act, 2002, shall continue to hold such office as President or member, as the case may be, till the completion of his term.

Jurisdiction of the State Commission.—(1) Subject to the other provisions of this Act, the State Commission shall have jurisdiction—

(a) to entertain—

(i) complaints where the value of the goods or services and compensation, if any, claimed exceeds rupees twenty lakhs but does not exceed rupees one crore; and

(ii) appeals against the orders of any District Forum within the State; and

(b) to call for the records and pass appropriate orders in any consumer dispute which is pending before or has been decided by any District Forum within the State, where it appears to the State Commission that such District Forum has exercised a jurisdiction not vested in it by law, or has failed to exercise a jurisdiction so vested or has acted in exercise of its jurisdiction illegally or with material irregularity.

Filing a complaint with State Commission.—A complaint shall be instituted in a State Commission within the limits of whose jurisdiction,—

(a) the opposite party or each of the opposite parties, where there are more than one, at the time of the institution of the complaint, actually and voluntarily resides or carries on business or has a branch office or personally works for gain; or

(b) any of the opposite parties, where there are more than one, at the time of the institution of the complaint, actually and voluntarily resides, or carries on business or has a branch office or personally works for gain, provided that in such case either the permission of the State Commission is given or the opposite parties who do not reside or carry on business or have a branch office or personally work for gain, as the case may be, acquiesce in such institution; or

(c) the cause of action, wholly or in part, arises.

Transfer of cases.—On the application of the complainant or of its own motion, the State Commission may, at any stage of the proceeding, transfer any complaint pending before the District Forum to another District Forum within the State if the interest of justice so requires.

Circuit Benches.—The State Commission shall ordinarily function in the State Capital but may perform its functions at such other place as the State Government may, in consultation with the State Commission, notify in the Official Gazette, from time to time.

Procedure applicable to State Commissions.—The provisions of Sections 12, 13 and 14 and the rules made thereunder for the disposal of complaints by the District Forum shall, with such modifications as may be necessary, be applicable to the disposal of disputes by the State Commission.

Appeals.—Any person aggrieved by an order made by the State Commission in exercise of its powers conferred by sub-clause (i) of clause (a) of section 17 may prefer an appeal against such order to the National Commission within a period of thirty days from the date of the order in such form and manner as may be prescribed:

Provided that the National Commission may entertain an appeal after the expiry of the said period of thirty days if it is satisfied that there was sufficient cause for not filing it within that period:

Provided further that no appeal by a person, who is required to pay any amount in terms of an order of the State Commission, shall be entertained by the National Commission unless the appellant has deposited in the prescribed manner fifty per cent of the amount or rupees thirty-five thousand, whichever is less:

Hearing of Appeal—An appeal filed before the State Commission or the National Commission shall be heard as expeditiously as possible and an endeavour shall be made to finally dispose of the appeal within a period of ninety days from the date of its admission:

Provided that no adjournment shall be ordinarily granted by the State Commission or the National Commission, as the case may be, unless sufficient cause is shown and the reasons for grant of adjournment have been recorded in writing by such Commission:

Provided further that the State Commission or the National Commission, as the case may be, shall make such orders as to the costs occasioned by the adjournment as may be provided in the regulations made under this Act:

Provided also that in the event of an appeal being disposed of after the period so specified, the State Commission or, the

National Commission, as the case may be, shall record in writing the reasons for the same at the time of disposing of the said appeal.

8.9 COMPOSITION OF THE NATIONAL COMMISSION

Composition of the National Commission.—(1) The National Commission shall consist of—

(a) a person who is or has been a Judge of the Supreme Court, to be appointed by the Central Government, who shall be its President:

Provided that no appointment under this clause shall be made except after consultation with the Chief Justice of India;

(b) not less than four, and not more than such number of members, as may be prescribed, and one of whom shall be a woman, who shall have the following qualifications, namely:—

(i) be not less than thirty-five years of age;

(ii) possess a bachelor's degree from a recognised university; and

(iii) be persons of ability, integrity and standing and have adequate knowledge and experience of at least ten years in dealing with problems relating to economics, law, commerce, accountancy, industry, public affairs or administration:

Provided that not more than fifty per cent of the members shall be from amongst the persons having a judicial background.

Explanation.—For the purposes of this clause, the expression "persons having judicial background" shall mean persons having knowledge and experience for at least a period of ten years as a presiding officer at the district level court or any tribunal at equivalent level:

Provided further that a person shall be disqualified for appointment, if he—

(a) has been convicted and sentenced to imprisonment for an offence which, in the opinion of the Central Government, involves moral turpitude; or

(b) is an undischarged insolvent; or

(c) is of unsound mind and stands so declared by a

competent court; or

(d) has been removed or dismissed from the service of the Government or a body corporate owned or controlled by the Government; or

(e) has in the opinion of the Central Government such financial or other interest as is likely to affect prejudicially the discharge by him of his functions as a member; or

(f) has such other disqualifications as may be prescribed by the Central Government:

Provided also that every appointment under this clause shall be made by the Central Government on the recommendation of a selection committee consisting of the following, namely:—

(a) a person who is a Judge of the Supreme Court, to be nominated by the Chief Justice of India—Chairman;

(b) the Secretary in the Department of Legal Affairs in the Government of India—Member;

(c) Secretary of the Department dealing with consumer affairs in the Government of India —Member.

(1A) (i) The jurisdiction, powers and authority of the National Commission may be exercised by Benches thereof.

(ii) A Bench may be constituted by the President with one or more members as the President may deem fit.

(iii) If the Members of a Bench differ in opinion on any point, the points shall be decided according to the opinion of the majority, if there is a majority, but if the members are equally divided, they shall state the point or points on which they differ, and make a reference to the President who shall either hear the point or points himself or refer the case for hearing on such point or points by one or more or the other Members and such point or points shall be decided according to the opinion of the majority of the Members who have heard the case, including those who first heard it.

(2) The salary or honorarium and other allowances payable to and the other terms and conditions of service of the members of the National Commission shall be such as may be prescribed by the Central Government.

(3) Every member of the National Commission shall hold office for a term of five years or up to the age of seventy years, whichever is earlier:

Provided that a member shall be eligible for re-appointment for another term of five years or up to the age of seventy years, whichever is earlier, subject to the condition that he fulfils the qualifications and other conditions for appointment mentioned in clause (b) of sub-section (1) and such re-appointment is made on the basis of the recommendation of the Selection Committee:

Provided further that a person appointed as a President of the National Commission shall also be eligible for re-appointment in the manner provided in clause (a) of sub-section (1):

Provided also that a member may resign his office in writing under his hand addressed to the Central Government and on such resignation being accepted, his office shall become vacant and may be filled by appointment of a person possessing any of the qualifications mentioned in sub-section (1) in relation to the category of the member who is required to be appointed under the provisions of sub-section (1A) in place of the person who has resigned.

(4) Notwithstanding anything contained in sub-section (3), a person appointed as a President or as a member before the commencement of the Consumer Protection (Amendment) Act, 2002 shall continue to hold such office as President or member, as the case may be, till the completion of his term.

Jurisdiction of the National Commission.—Subject to the other provisions of this Act, the National Commission shall have jurisdiction—

(a) to entertain—
   (i) complaints where the value of the goods or services and compensation, if any, claimed exceeds rupees one crore; and
   (ii) appeals against the orders of any State Commission;

(b) to call for the records and pass appropriate orders in any consumer dispute which is pending before or has been decided by any State Commission where it appears to the National Commission that such State Commission has exercised a jurisdiction not vested in it by law, or has failed to exercise a jurisdiction so vested, or has acted in the exercise of its jurisdiction illegally or with material irregularity.

Power of and procedure applicable to the National Commission.—(1) The provisions of sections 12, 13 and 14 and the rules made thereunder for the disposal of complaints by the District Forum shall, with such modifications as may be considered necessary by the Commission, be applicable to the disposal of disputes by the National Commission.

(2) Without prejudice to the provisions contained in sub-section (1), the National Commission shall have the power to review any order made by it, when there is an error apparent on the face of record.

Power to set aside ex-parte orders.—Where an order is passed by the National Commission ex-parte against the opposite party or a complainant, as the case may be, the aggrieved party may apply to the Commission to set aside the said order in the interest of justice.

Transfer of cases—On the application of the complainant or of its own motion, the National Commission may, at any stage of the proceeding, in the interest of justice, transfer any complaint pending before the District Forum of one State to a District Forum of another State or before one State Commission to another State Commission.

Circuit Benches—The National Commission shall ordinarily function at New Delhi and perform its functions at such other place as the Central Government may, in consultation with the National Commission, notify in the Official Gazette, from time to time.

Vacancy in the Office of the President—When the office of President of a District Forum, State Commission, or of the National Commission, as the case may be, is vacant or a person occupying such office is, by reason of absence or otherwise, unable to perform the duties of his office, these shall be performed by the senior-most member of the District Forum, the State Commission or of the National Commission, as the case may be:

Provided that where a retired Judge of a High Court is a member of the National Commission, such member or where the number of such members are more than one, the senior-most person among such members, shall preside over the National Commission in the absence of President of that Commission.

8.10 APPEAL

Any person, aggrieved by an order made by the National Commission in exercise of its powers conferred by sub-clause (i) of clause (a) of section 21, may prefer an appeal against such order of the Supreme Court within a period of thirty days from the date of the order:

> Provided that the Supreme Court may entertain an appeal after the expiry of the said period of thirty days if it is satisfied that there was sufficient cause for not filing it within that period.
>
> Provided further that no appeal by a person who is required to pay any amount in terms of an order of the National Commission shall be entertained by the Supreme Court unless that person has deposited in the prescribed manner fifty per cent of that amount or rupees fifty thousand, whichever is less.

Finality of orders.—Every order of a District Forum, the State Commission or the National Commission shall, if no appeal has been preferred against such order under the provisions of this Act, be final.

Limitation period.—(l) The District Forum, the State Commission or the National Commission shall not admit a complaint unless it is filed within two years from the date on which the cause of action has arisen.

(2) Notwithstanding anything contained in sub-section (1), a complaint may be entertained after the period specified in sub-section (l), if the complainant satisfies the District Forum, the State Commission or the National Commission, as the case may be, that he had sufficient cause for not filing the complaint within such period:

> Provided that no such complaint shall be entertained unless the National Commission, the State Commission or the District Forum, as the case may be, records its reasons for condoning such delay.

Administrative Control.—(1) The National Commission shall have administrative control over all the State Commissions in the following matters, namely:—

(i) calling for periodical return regarding the institution, disposal pendency of cases;

(ii) issuance of instructions regarding adoption of uniform

procedure in the hearing of matters, prior service of copies of documents produced by one party to the opposite parties, furnishing of English translation of judgments written in any language, speedy grant of copies of documents; and

(iii) generally overseeing the functioning of the State Commissions or the District Fora to ensure that the objects and purposes of the Act are best served without in any way interfering with their quasi-judicial freedom.

(2) The State Commission shall have administrative control over all the District Fora within its jurisdiction in all matters referred to in sub-section (1).

Enforcement of orders of the District Forum, the State Commission or the National Commission.—(1) Where an interim order made under this Act, is not complied with the District Forum or the State Commission or the National Commission, as the case may be, may order the property of the person, not complying with such order to be attached.

(2) No attachment made under sub-section (1) shall remain in force for more than three months at the end of which, if the non-compliance continues, the property attached may be sold and out of the proceeds thereof, the District Forum or the State Commission or the National Commission may award such damages as it thinks fit to the complainant and shall pay the balance, if any, to the party entitled thereto.

(3) Where any amount is due from any person under an order made by a District Forum, State Commission or the National Commission, as the case may be, the person entitled to the amount may make an application to the District Forum, the State Commission or the National Commission, as the case may be, and such District Forum or the State Commission or the National Commission may issue a certificate for the said amount to the Collector of the district (by whatever name called) and the Collector shall proceed to recover the amount in the same manner as arrears of land revenue.

Dismissal of frivolous or vexatious complaints.—Where a complaint instituted before the District Forum, the State Commission or as the case may be, the National Commission, is found to be frivolous or vexatious, it shall, for reasons to be recorded in writing, dismiss the complaint and make an order that the complainant shall pay to the opposite party such cost, not exceeding ten thousand rupees, as may be specified in the order

8.11 PENALTIES

Penalties.—(1) Where a trader or a person against whom a complaint is made or the complainant fails or omits to comply with any order made by the District Forum, the State Commission or the National Commission, as the case may be, such trader or person or complainant shall be punishable with imprisonment for a term which shall not be less than one month but which may extend to three years, or with fine which shall not be less than two thousands rupees but which may extend to ten thousand rupees, or with both.

(2) Notwithstanding anything contained in the Code of Criminal Procedure, 1973 (2 of 1974), the District Forum or the State Commission or the National Commission, as the case may be, shall have the power of a Judicial Magistrate of the first class for the trial of offences under this Act, and on such conferment of powers, the District Forum or the State Commission or the National Commission, as the case may be, on whom the powers are so conferred, shall be deemed to be a Judicial Magistrate of the first class for the purpose of the Code of Criminal Procedure, 1973 (2 of 1974).

(3) All offences under this Act may be tried summarily by the District Forum or the State Commission or the National Commission, as the case may be.

Appeal against order passed under section 27—(1) Notwithstanding anything contained in the Code of Criminal Procedure, 1973 (2 of 1974), an appeal under section 27, both on facts and on law, shall lie from—

(a) the order made by the District Forum to the State Commission;
(b) the order made by the State Commission to the National Commission; and
(c) the order made by the National Commission to the Supreme Court.

(2) Except as aforesaid, no appeal shall lie to any court from any order of a District Forum or a State Commission or the National Commission.

(3) Every appeal under this section shall be preferred within a

period of thirty days from the date of an order of a District Forum or a State Commission or, as the case may be, the National Commission:

Provided that the State Commission or the National Commission or the Supreme Court, as the case may be, may entertain an appeal after the expiry of the said period of thirty days, if, it is satisfied that the appellant had sufficient cause for not preferring the appeal within the period of thirty days.

8.12 MISCELLANEOUS

Protection of action taken in good faith.—No suit, prosecution or other legal proceedings shall lie against the members of the District Forum, the State Commission or the National Commission or any officer or person acting under the direction of the District Forum, the State Commission or the National Commission for executing any order made by it or in respect of anything which is in good faith done or intended to be done by such member, officer or person under this Act or under any rule or order made thereunder.

Service of notice, etc.—(1) All notices required by this Act to be served shall be served in the manner hereinafter mentioned in sub-section (2).

(2) The service of notices may be made by delivering or transmitting a copy thereof by registered post acknowledgment due addressed to opposite party against whom complaint is made or to the complainant by speed post or by such courier service as are approved by the District Forum, the State Commission or the National Commission, as the case may be, or by any other means of transmission of documents (including FAX message).

(3) When an acknowledgment or any other receipt purporting to be signed by the opposite party or his agent or by the complainant is received by the District Forum, the State Commission or the National Commission, as the case may be, or postal article containing the notice is received back by such District Forum, State Commission or the National Commission, with an endorsement purporting to have been made by a postal employee or by any person authorized by the courier service to the effect that the opposite party or his agent or complainant had refused to take delivery of the postal article containing the notice or had refused to accept the notice by any other means specified in sub-section (2) when tendered or transmitted to him, the District

Forum or the State Commission or the National Commission, as the case may be, shall declare that the notice had been duly served on the opposite party or to the complainant:

Provided that where the notice was properly addressed, pre-paid and duly sent by registered post acknowledgment due, a declaration referred to in this sub-section shall be made notwithstanding the fact that the acknowledgment has been lost or mislaid, or for any other reason, has not been received by the District Forum, the State Commission or the National Commission, as the case may be, within thirty days from the date of issue of notice.

(4) All notices required to be served on an opposite party or to complainant shall be deemed to be sufficiently served, if addressed in the case of the opposite party to the place where business or profession is carried and in case of complainant, the place where such person actually and voluntarily resides.

Power to remove difficulties.—(1) If any difficulty arises in giving effect to the provisions of this Act, the (Central Government may, by order in the official Gazette, make such provisions not inconsistent with the provisions of this Act as appear to it to be necessary or expedient for removing the difficulty:

Provided that no such order shall be made after the expiry of a period of two years from the commencement of this Act.

(2) Every order made under this section shall, as soon as may be after it is made be laid before each House of Parliament.

(3) If any difficulty arises in giving effect to the provisions of the Consumer Protection (Amendment) Act, 2002, the Central Government may, by order, do anything not inconsistent with such provisions for the purpose of removing the difficulty:

Provided that no such order shall be made after the expiry of a period of two years from the commencement of the Consumer Protection (Amendment) Act, 2002.

(4) Every order made under sub-section (3) shall be laid before each House of Parliament.

Vacancies or defects in appointment not to invalidate orders.—No act or proceeding of the District Forum, the State Commission or the National Commission shall be invalid by reason only of the existence of any vacancy amongst its member or any defect in the constitution thereof.

Power to make rules.—(1) The Central Government may, by notification, make rules for carrying out the provisions contained in clause (a) of sub-section (1) of section 2, clause (b) of sub-section (2) of section 4, sub-section (2) of section 5, sub-section (2) of section 12, clause (vi) of sub-section (4) of section 13, clause (hb) of sub-section (1) of section 14, section 19, clause (b) of sub-section (1) and sub-section (2) of section 20, section 22 and section 23 of this Act.

(2) The State Government may, by notification, make rules for carrying out the provisions contained in clause (b) of sub-section (2) and sub-section (4) of section 7, clause (b) of sub-section (2) and sub-section (4) of section 8A, clause (b) of sub-section (1) and sub-section (3) of section 10, clause (c) of sub-section (1) of section 13 clause (hb) of sub-section (1) and sub-section (3) of section 14, section 15 and clause (b) of sub-section (1) and sub-section (2) of section 16 of this Act.

Power of the National Commission to make regulations—(1) The National Commission may, with the previous approval of the Central Government, by notification, make regulations not inconsistent with this Act to provide for all matters for which provision is necessary or expedient for the purpose of giving effect to the provisions of this Act.

(2) In particular and without prejudice to the generality of the foregoing power, such regulations may make provisions for the cost of adjournment of any proceeding before the District Forum, the State Commission or the National Commission, as the case may be, which a party may be ordered to pay.

Rules and regulations to be laid before each House of Parliament.—(1) Every rule and every regulation made under this Act shall be laid, as soon as may be after it is made, before each House of Parliament, while it is in session, for a total period of thirty days which may be comprised in one session or in two or more successive sessions, and if, before the expiry of the session immediately following the session or the successive sessions aforesaid, both Houses agree in making any modification in the rule or regulation or both Houses agree that the rule or regulation should not be made, the rule or regulation shall thereafter have effect only in such modified form or be of no effect, as the case may be; so, however, that any such modification or annulment shall be without prejudice to the validity of anything previously done under that rule or regulation.

(2) Every rule made by a State Government under this Act shall be laid as soon as may be after it is made, before the State Legislature.

8.13 CONCLUSION

Consumer Protection Act was enacted in 1986 to promote and protect consumer's interests against exploitation and unfair trade practices adopted by the producers.

The Act gives six rights to consumers. These are:

- Right to safety
- Right to information
- Right to choice
- Right to consumer education
- Right to seek redressal
- Right to be heard/Right to representation.

Consumer Protection Councils have been established at three levels to protect the interest of the consumers.

- Central Consumer Protection Council
- State Consumer Protection Council
- District Consumer Protection Council

Consumer Dispute Redressal Agencies have been established in three tier structure where a consumer can file a complaint and seek redressal against the unfair trade practices of the producers and sellers:

- District Forum
- State Commission
- National Commission

Appeal both on facts and on law, shall lie from—

- the order made by the District Forum to the State Commission;
- the order made by the State Commission to the National Commission; and
- the order made by the National Commission to the Supreme Court.

Short Questions

1. State the objective of the act.
2. Who under the act can file a complaint?
3. Defines the following terms:
   a. complainant; b. complaint; and c. consumer
4. Define the following terms:
   a. deficiency; b. service; c. manufacture; d. restrictive trade practice; and e. circuit benches

Long Questions

1. What are the objects of the Consumer Protection Act, 1986?
2. Define the following terms as used in the Consumer Protection Act, 1986: Complaint, Complainant, Consumer, Manufacturer, Restrictive trade practice, unfair trade practice.
3. What are the objects of the Central Consumer Protection Council?
4. What is the function of the State Consumer Protection Council?
5. Write a note on: The Consumer Disputes Redressal Agencies.
6. What is the jurisdiction of Consumer Disputes Redressal Forum (the District Forum)? In what manner is a complaint filed before it? What procedure is followed by it after receiving a complaint?
7. Write a note on: Consumer Disputes Redressal Commission (the State Commission) as to its composition, jurisdiction and procedure to be followed by it.
8. What is the composition of the National Consumer Disputes Redressal Commission (the National Commission) ? What is its jurisdiction and what procedure does it follow to settle any complaint?

Practical Problems

- A consumer's cheque was dishounoured by a blank inspite of the sufficient balance in the account. Is the bank liable under the consumer Protection Act?

  [P.U. B.Com. 2012]

  [*Hint:* Yes, the bank is liable as it amount to deficiency in service.]
- The telephone connection of a customer was disconnected for non-payment of disputed bill without referring the matter to arbitration. Is the Telecom Deptt. of BSNL liable?
  [*Hint:* Yes, it amounts to deficiency in service.]

- X, a driver purchased a taxi car as a self-employed operator. The car had a manufacturing defect. X filed a suit for the recovery of Rs. 20,000 for removing the manufacturer defect? The manufacturer denied the liability on the ground that X is not a consumer.
  [*Hint:* The manufacturer is liable to pay as X is a consumer.]

9

THE ENVIRONMENT (PROTECTION) ACT, 1986

LEARNING OBJECTIVES

- 9.1 Definitions
- 9.2 Objective and Scope of the Environment (Protection) Act, 1986
- 9.3 Powers Provided by the Act to Central Government
- 9.4 Appointment of Officers and their Powers and Functions
- 9.5. Power to give Directions
- 9.6 Rules to Regulate Environmental Pollution
- 9.7 Prevention, Control, and Abatement of Environmental Pollution
- 9.8. Persons Handling Hazardous Substances to Comply with Procedural Safeguards
- 9.9 Furnishing of Information to Authorities and Agencies in Certain Cases
- 9.10. Powers of Entry and Inspection
- 9.11 Power to take Sample and Procedure to be followed in Connection Therewith
- 9.12 Environmental Laboratories
- 9.13 Government Analysts
- 9.14 Reports of Government Analysts

9.15 Penalty for Contravention of the Provisions of the Act and the Rules, Orders and Directions
9.16 Offences by Companies
9.17 Offences by Government Departments
9.18 Conclusion

In the wake of Bhopal tragedy, the Government of India enacted the Environment (Protection) Act, 1986 (EPA) under Article 253 of the constitution. The purpose of the Act is to act as an "umbrella" legislation designed to provide a framework for Central government co-ordination of the activities of various central and state authorities established under previous laws, such as Water Act and Air Act.

An Act to provide for the protection and improvement of environment and for matters connected therewith: whereas the decisions were taken at the united nations conference on the human environment held at Stockholm in June 1972, in which India participated, to take appropriate steps for the protection and improvement of human environment; and whereas it is considered necessary further to implement the decisions aforesaid in so far as they relate to the protection and improvement of environment and the prevention of hazards to human beings, other living creatures, plants and property; the Environment Protection Act, 1986 (in India) introduction.

In 1980, the Department of Environment was established in India. later on it became the ministry of environment and forests in 1985. EPA, 1986 came into force soon after the Bhopal gas tragedy.

9.1 DEFINITIONS

In this Act, unless the context otherwise requires,—

"Environment" It includes water, air, and land and the interrelationship which exists among and between water, air and land and human beings, other living creatures, plants, microorganism and property. "Environmental Pollutant" means any solid, liquid or gaseous substance present in such concentration as may be, or tend to be injurious to environment.

(a) **"Environmental pollutant"** means any solid, liquid or gaseous substances present in such concentration as may be or tend to be injurious to environment and human being. "Hazardous Substance" means any substance or preparation which, by reasons of its chemical or physico-chemical properties, is liable to cause harm to human beings or other living creatures. "Handling": in relation to any substance, it means the manufacturing, processing, treatment, packaging, storage, transportation, use, collection, destruction, conversion, offering for sale, etc.;

(b) **"Environmental pollution"** means imbalance in environment. The materials or substances when after mixing in air, water or land alters their properties in such manner, that the very use of all or any of the air, water and land by man and any other living organism becomes lethal and dangerous for health. "Occupier": It means a person who has control over the affairs of the factory or the premises, and includes, in relation to any substance, the person in possession of the substance;

(c) **"Hazardous substance"** means any substance or preparation which, by reason of its chemical or physico-chemical properties or handling, is liable to cause harm to human beings, other living creatures, plant, micro-organism, property or the environment;

(d) **"Handling"**, in relation to any substance, means the manufacture, processing, treatment, package, storage, transportation, use, collection, destruction, conversion, offering for sale, transfer or the like of such substance;

(e) **"Hazardous substance"** means any substance or preparation which, by reason of its chemical or physico-chemical properties or handling, is liable to cause harm to human beings, other living creatures, plant, micro-organism, property or the environment;

(f) **"Occupier"**, in relation to any factory or premises, means a person who has, control over the affairs of the factory or the premises and includes in relation to any substance, the person in possession of the substance;

(g) **"Prescribed"** means prescribed by rules made under this Act.

9.2 OBJECTIVE AND SCOPE OF THE ENVIRONMENT (PROTECTION) ACT, 1986

Objective is, to provide the protection and improvement of

environment. In EPA, Article 48A, specify that the State shall protect and improve the environment.

Also, to safeguard the forests and wildlife of the country. According to Sec. 51(A) every citizen shall protect the environment. EPA is applicable to whole India, including J&K.

The potential scope of the Act is broad, with "environment" defined to include water, air and land and the inter-relationships which exist among water, air and land, and human beings and other living creatures, plants, micro-organisms and property.

9.3 POWERS PROVIDED BY THE ACT TO CENTRAL GOVERNMENT

To make rules to regulate environmental pollution; To notify standards and maximum limits of pollutants of air, water, and soil for various areas and purposes; Prohibition and restriction on the handling of hazardous substances, and location of industries (Sections 3-6).

Under Sec. (3): may constitute authority or authorities for the purpose of exercising of performing such of the powers and functions; Under Sec. (4): may appoint a person for inspection; Under Sec. (5): may issue directions in writing to any officers or any authority to comply; Under Sec. (6): it empower the government to make rules to achieve the object of the Act.

Under Sec. (7): persons carrying on industry, operation, etc. not to allow emission or discharge of environmental pollutants in excess of the standards; Under Sec. (8): persons handling hazardous substances must comply with procedural safeguards.

Power of Central Government to take Measures to Protect and Improve Environment.—(1) Subject to the provisions of this Act, the Central Government, shall have the power to take all such measures as it deems necessary or expedient for the purpose of protecting and improving the quality of the environment and preventing controlling and abating environmental pollution.

(2) In particular, and without prejudice to the generality of the provisions of sub-section (1), such measures may include measures with respect to all or any of the following matters, namely:—

(i) co-ordination of actions by the State Governments, officers and other authorities—

(a) under this Act, or the rules made thereunder, or

(b) under any other law for the time being in force which is relatable to the objects of this Act;

(ii) planning and execution of a nation-wide programmed for the prevention, control and abatement of environmental pollution;

(iii) laying down standards for the quality of environment in its various aspects;

(iv) laying down standards for emission or discharge of environmental pollutants from various sources whatsoever:
Provided that different standards for emission or discharge may be laid down under this clause from different sources having regard to the quality or composition of the emission or discharge of environmental pollutants from such sources;

(v) restriction of areas in which any industries, operations or processes or class of industries, operations or processes shall not be carried out or shall be carried out subject to certain safeguards;

(vi) laying down procedures and safeguards for the prevention of accidents which may cause environmental pollution and remedial measures for such accidents;

(vii) laying down procedures and safeguards for the handling of hazardous substances;

(viii) examination of such manufacturing processes, materials and substances as are likely to cause environmental pollution;

(ix) carrying out and sponsoring investigations and research relating to problems of environmental pollution;

(x) inspection of any premises, plant, equipment, machinery, manufacturing or other processes, materials or substances and giving, by order, of such directions to such authorities, officers or persons as it may consider necessary to take steps for the prevention, control and abatement of environmental pollution;

(xi) establishment or recognition of environmental laboratories and institutes to carry out the functions entrusted to such environmental laboratories and institutes under this Act;

(xii) collection and dissemination of information in respect of matters relating to environmental pollution;

(xiii) preparation of manuals, codes or guides relating to the prevention, control and abatement of environmental pollution; and

(xiv) such other matters as the Central Government deems necessary or expedient for the purpose of securing the effective implementation of the provisions of this Act.

(3) The Central Government may, if it considers it necessary or expedient so to do for the purpose of this Act, by order, published in the Official Gazette, constitute an authority or authorities by such name or names as may be specified in the order for the purpose of exercising and performing such of the powers and functions (including the power to issue directions under section 5) of the Central Government under this Act and for taking measures with respect to such of the matters referred to in sub-section (2) as may be mentioned in the order and subject to the supervision and control of the Central Government and the provisions of such order, such authority or authorities may exercise and powers or perform the functions or take the measures so mentioned in the order as if such authority or authorities had been empowered by this Act to exercise those powers or perform measures.

9.4 APPOINTMENT OF OFFICERS AND THEIR POWERS AND FUNCTIONS

(1) Without prejudice to the provisions of sub-section (3) of section 3, the Central Government may appoint officers with such designation as it thinks fit for the purposes of this Act and may entrust to them such of the powers and functions under this Act as it may deem fit.

(2) The officers appointed under sub-section (1) shall be subject to the general control and direction of the Central Government or, if so directed by that Government, also of the authority or authorities, if any, constituted under sub-section (3) of section 3 or of any other authority or officer.

9.5. POWER TO GIVE DIRECTIONS

Notwithstanding anything contained in any other law but subject to the provisions of this Act, the Central Government may, in the exercise of its powers and performance of its functions under this Act, issue directions in writing to any person, officer or any authority and such person, officer or authority shall be bound to comply with such directions.

Explanation—For the avoidance of doubts, it is hereby declared that the power to issue directions under this section includes the power to direct—

(a) the closure, prohibition or regulation of any industry, operation or process; or

(b) stoppage or regulation of the supply of electricity or water or any other service.

9.6 RULES TO REGULATE ENVIRONMENTAL POLLUTION

(1) The Central Government may, by notification in the Official Gazette, make rules in respect of all or any of the matters referred to in section 3.

(2) In particular, and without prejudice to the generality of the foregoing power, such rules may provide for all or any of the following matters, namely:—

(a) the standards of quality of air, water or soil for various areas and purposes;

(b) the maximum allowable limits of concentration of various environmental pollutants (including noise) for different areas;

(c) the procedures and safeguards for the handling of hazardous substances;

(d) the prohibition and restrictions on the handling of hazardous substances in different areas;

(e) the prohibition and restriction on the location of industries and the carrying on process and operations in different areas;7

(f) the procedures and safeguards for the prevention of accidents which may cause environmental pollution and for providing for remedial measures for such accidents.

9.7 PREVENTION, CONTROL, AND ABATEMENT OF ENVIRONMENTAL POLLUTION

Persons Carrying on Industry Operation, etc., not to Allow Emission or Discharge of Environmental Pollutants in Excess of the Standards.—No person carrying on any industry, operation or process shall discharge or emit or permit to be discharged or emitted any environmental pollutants in excess of such standards as may be prescribed.

9.8. PERSONS HANDLING HAZARDOUS SUBSTANCES TO COMPLY WITH PROCEDURAL SAFEGUARDS

No person shall handle or cause to be handled any hazardous substance except in accordance with such procedure and after complying with such safeguards as may be prescribed.

9.9 FURNISHING OF INFORMATION TO AUTHORITIES AND AGENCIES IN CERTAIN CASES

(1) Where the discharge of any environmental pollutant in excess of the prescribed standards occurs or is apprehended to occur due to any accident or other unforeseen act or event, the person responsible for such discharge and the person in charge of the place at which such discharge occurs or is apprehended to occur shall be bound to prevent or mitigate the environmental pollution caused as a result of such discharge and shall also forthwith—

(a) intimate the fact of such occurrence or apprehension of such occurrence; and

(b) be bound, if called upon, to render all assistance,

to such authorities or agencies as may be prescribed.

(2) On receipt of information with respect to the fact or apprehension on any occurrence of the nature referred to in sub-section (1), whether through intimation under that sub-section or otherwise, the authorities or agencies referred to in sub-section (1) shall, as early as practicable, cause such remedial measures to be taken as necessary to prevent or mitigate the environmental pollution.

(3) The expenses, if any, incurred by any authority or agency with respect to the remedial measures referred to in sub-section (2), together with interest (at such reasonable rate as the Government may, by order, fix) from the date when a demand for the expenses is made until it is paid, may be recovered by such authority or agency from the person concerned as arrears of land revenue or of public demand.

9.10. POWERS OF ENTRY AND INSPECTION

(1) Subject to the provisions of this section, any person empowered by the Central Government in this behalf shall have a right to enter,

at all reasonable times with such assistance as he considers necessary, any place—

(a) for the purpose of performing any of the functions of the Central Government entrusted to him;

(b) for the purpose of determining whether and if so in what manner, any such functions are to be performed or whether any provisions of this Act or the rules made thereunder or any notice, order, direction or authorization served, made, given or granted under this Act is being or has been complied with; and

(c) for the purpose of examining and testing any equipment, industrial plant, record, register, document or any other material object or for conducting a search of any building in which he has reason to believe that an offence under this Act or the rules made thereunder has been or is being or is about to be committed and for seizing any such equipment, industrial plant, record, register, document or other material object if he has reason to believe that it may furnish evidence of the commission of an offence punishable under this Act or the rules made thereunder or that such seizure is necessary to prevent or mitigate environmental pollution.

(2) Every person carrying on any industry, operation or process of handling any hazardous substance shall be bound to render all assistance to the person empowered by the Central Government under sub-section (1) for carrying out the functions under that sub-section and if he fails to do so without any reasonable cause or excuse, he shall be guilty of an offence under this Act.

(3) If any person will fully delays or obstructs any persons empowered by the Central Government under sub-section (1) in the performance of his functions, he shall be guilty of an offence under this Act.

(4) The provisions of the Code of Criminal Procedure, 1973, or, in relation to the State of Jammu and Kashmir, or an area in which that Code is not in force, the provisions of any corresponding law in force in that State or area shall, so far as may be, apply to any search or seizures under this section as they apply to any search or seizure made under the authority of a warrant issued under section 94 of the said Code or as the case may be, under the corresponding provision of the said law.

9.11 POWER TO TAKE SAMPLE AND PROCEDURE TO BE FOLLOWED IN CONNECTION THEREWITH

(1) The Central Government or any officer empowered by it in this behalf, shall have power to take, for the purpose of analysis, samples of air, water, soil or other substance from any factory, premises or other place in such manner as may be prescribed.

(2) The result of any analysis of a sample taken under sub-section (1) shall not be admissible in evidence in any legal proceeding unless the provisions of sub-sections (3) and (4) are complied with.

(3) Subject to the provisions of sub-section (4), the person taking the sample under sub-section (1) shall—

(a) serve on the occupier or his agent or person in-charge of the place, a notice, then and there, in such form as may be prescribed, of his intention to have it so analyses;

(b) in the presence of the occupier of his agent or person, collect a sample for analysis;

(c) cause the sample to be placed in a container or containers which shall be marked and sealed and shall also be signed both by the person taking the sample and the occupier or his agent or person; and

(d) send without delay, the container or the containers to the laboratory established or recognized by the Central Government under section 12.

(4) When a sample is taken for analysis under sub-section (1) and the person taking the sample serves on the occupier or his agent or person, a notice under clause (a) of sub-section (3), then,—

(a) in a case where the occupier, his agent or person will fully absents himself, the person taking the sample shall collect the sample for analysis to be placed in a container or containers which shall be marked and sealed and shall also be signed by the person taking the sample, and

(b) in a case where the occupier or his agent or person present at the time of taking the sample refuses to sign the marked and sealed container or containers of the sample as required under clause (c) of sub-section (3), the marked and sealed container or containers shall be signed by the person taking the samples, and the container or containers shall be sent without delay by the person taking the sample for analysis to the laboratory established or recognized under section 12 and such person shall inform the Government Analyst appointed or recognized under section 12 in writing, about the wilful absence of the occupier or his agent or person, or, as the case may be, his refusal to sign the container or containers.

9.12 ENVIRONMENTAL LABORATORIES

(1) The Central Government may, by notification in the Official Gazette,—

(a) establish one or more environmental laboratories; and
(b) recognize one or more laboratories or institutes as environmental laboratories to carry out the functions entrusted to an environmental laboratory under this Act.

(2) The Central Government may, by notification in the Official Gazette, make rules specifying—

(a) the functions of the environmental laboratory;
(b) the procedure for the submission to the said laboratory of samples of air, water, soil or other substance for analysis or tests, the form of the laboratory report thereon and the fees payable for such report; and
(c) such other matters as may be necessary or expedient to enable that laboratory to carry out its functions.

9.13 GOVERNMENT ANALYSTS

The Central Government may by notification in the Official Gazette, appoint or recognize such persons as it thinks fit and having the prescribed qualifications to be Government Analysts for the purpose of analysis of samples of air, water, soil or other substance sent for analysis to any environmental laboratory established or recognized under sub-section (1) of section 12.

9.14 REPORTS OF GOVERNMENT ANALYSTS

Any document purporting to be a report signed by a Government analyst may be used as evidence of the facts stated therein in any proceeding under this Act.

9.15 PENALTY FOR CONTRAVENTION OF THE PROVISIONS OF THE ACT AND THE RULES, ORDERS AND DIRECTIONS

(1) Whoever fails to comply with or contravenes any of the provisions of this Act, or the rules made or orders or directions issued thereunder, shall, in respect of each such failure or contravention, be punishable with imprisonment for a term which may extend to five years with fine which may extend to one lakh rupees, or with both, and in case the failure or contravention continues, with additional fine which may extend to five thousand rupees for every day during which such failure or contravention continues after the conviction for the first such failure or contravention.

(2) If the failure or contravention referred to in sub-section (1) continues beyond a period of one year after the date of conviction, the offender shall be punishable with imprisonment for a term which may extend to seven years.

9.16 OFFENCES BY COMPANIES

(1) Where any offence under this Act has been committed by a company, every person who, at the time the offence was committed, was directly in-charge of, and was responsible to, the company for the conduct of the business of the company, as well as the company, shall be deemed to be guilty of the offence and shall be liable to be proceeded against and punished accordingly:

Provided that nothing contained in this sub-section shall render any such person liable to any punishment provided in this Act, if he proves that the offence was committed without his knowledge or that he exercised all due diligence to prevent the commission of such offence.

(2) Notwithstanding anything contained in sub-section (1), where an offence under this Act has been committed by a company and it is proved that the offence has been committed with the consent or connivance of, or is attributable to any neglect on the part of, any director, manager, secretary or other officer of the company, such director, manager, secretary or other officer shall also deemed to be guilty of that offence and shall be liable to be proceeded against and punished accordingly.

Explanation—For the purpose of this section,—

(a) "company" means any body corporate and includes a firm or other association of individuals; and

(b) "director", in relation to a firm, means a partner in the firm.

9.17 OFFENCES BY GOVERNMENT DEPARTMENTS

(1) Where an offence under this Act has been committed by any Department of Government, the Head of the Department shall be deemed to be guilty of the offence and shall be liable to be proceeded against and punished accordingly.

Provided that nothing contained in this section shall render such Head of the Department liable to any punishment if he proves that the offence was committed without his knowledge or that he exercise all due diligence to prevent the commission of such offence.

(2) Notwithstanding anything contained in sub-section (1), where an offence under this Act has been committed by a Department of Government and it is proved that the offence has been committed with the consent or connivance of, or is attributable to any neglect on the part of, any officer, other than the Head of the Department, such officer shall also be deemed to be guilty of that offence and shall be liable to be proceeded against and punished accordingly.

9.18 CONCLUSION

1. Environment Protection Act came into force in 1986 after the Bhopal Gas tragedy.
2. The objective of EPA, 1986 is to provide the protection and safeguard the forests and wildlife of the country.
3. Central Government takes effective measures to protect and improve environment by laying down the standards for the quality of environmental pollutants from various sources.
4. Central Government appoint officers with such designation as it thinks fit for the purposes of Act and laid down proper rules to regulate environmental pollution.
5. Central Government shall have a right to enter, at all reasonable times and inspect, examining and testing any equipment, industrial plant, record, register, document to prevent environmental pollution.
6. Central Government shall establish one or more environmental laboratories to have samples of air, water, soil or other substance for tests and analysis.

Test Questions

1. What is the objective of the Environment Protection Act, 1986?
2. Discuss the scope and scheme of regulation under the Environment Protection Act, 1986.
3. Explain the following terms.
   (a) Environment
   (b) Environment pollutant
   (c) Environment pollution
   (d) Hazardous substance
   (e) Occupier
4. Enumerate the powers of the Central Government under the Environment Protection Act, 1986.
5. Summarise the provisions as regards prevention, control and abatement of environmental pollution.
6. What are the environmental laboratories? What are their functions?

10

RIGHT TO INFORMATION ACT, 2005

LEARNING OBJECTIVES

10.1 Introduction
10.2 Definitions
10.3 Scope and Extent
10.4 Right to Information and Obligations of Public Authorities
10.5 Powers and Functions of the Information Commissions, Appeal and Penalties
10.6 Conclusion

10.1 INTRODUCTION

The Right to Information Bill was introduced in the Lok Sabha in December 2004. It was passed by both the houses of Parliament in May 2005. The assent of the President was received on 15th June and the Act was notified in 'The Gazette of India, on 21st June, 2005. The Right to Information Act will become operational by the 12th October 2005 after the completion of 120 days from the date of Presidential assent. The Freedom of Information Act passed by the Parliament in 2002 has been repealed.

The citizens' right to information is not explicitly mentioned in the fundamental rights chapter of the Constitution. But in more than 10 cases the Supreme Court of India has declared that the fundamental right to life and liberty [Art. 21] and the fundamental right to freedom of speech and expression [Art. 19(1)] include every citizen's fundamental right to access information. Parliament passed the RTI Act to enable all citizens to use their fundamental right to access information from public bodies.

10.2 DEFINITIONS

1. Definitions.—(1) This Act may be called the Right to Information Act, 2005.

(2) It extends to the whole of India except the State of Jammu and Kashmir.

(3) The provisions of sub-section (*1*) of section 4, sub-sections (*1*) and (*2*) of section 5, sections 12, 13, 15,16, 24, 27 and 28 shall come into force at once, and the remaining provisions of this Act shall come into force on the one hundred and twentieth day of its enactment.

2. In this Act, unless the context otherwise requires.—(a) "**Appropriate Government**" means in relation to a public authority which is established, constituted, owned, controlled or substantially financed by funds provided directly or indirectly—

- (i) by the Central Government or the Union territory administration, the Central Government;
- (ii) by the State Government, the State Government;

(b) "**Central Information Commission**" means the Central Information Commission constituted under sub-section (*1*) of section 12;

(c) "**Central Public Information Officer**" means the Central Public Information Officer designated under sub-section (*1*) and includes a Central Assistant Public Information Officer designated as such under sub-section (*2*) of section 5;

(d) "**Chief Information Commissioner**" and "**Information Commissioner**" mean the Chief Information Commissioner and Information Commissioner appointed under sub-section (*3*) of section 12;

(e) "**Competent authority**" means—

- (i) the Speaker in the case of the House of the People or the Legislative Assembly of a State or a Union territory having such Assembly and the Chairman in the case of the Council of States or Legislative Council of a State;

(ii) the Chief Justice of India in the case of the Supreme Court;

(iii) the Chief Justice of the High Court in the case of a High Court;

(iv) the President or the Governor, as the case may be, in the case of other authorities established or constituted by or under the Constitution;

(v) the administrator appointed under Article 239 of the Constitution;

(f) "**Information**" means any material in any form, including records, documents, memos, e-mails, opinions, advices, press releases, circulars, orders, logbooks, contracts, reports, papers, samples, models, data material held in any electronic form and information relating to any private body which can be accessed by a public authority under any other law for the time being in force;

(g) "**Prescribed**" means prescribed by rules made under this Act by the appropriate Government or the competent authority, as the case may be;

(h) "**Public authority**" means any authority or body or institution of self-government established or constituted—

(a) by or under the Constitution;

(b) by any other law made by Parliament;

(c) by any other law made by State Legislature;

(d) by notification issued or order made by the appropriate Government, and includes any—

(i) body owned, controlled or substantially financed;

(ii) non-Government organization substantially financed, directly or indirectly by funds provided by the appropriate Government;

(i) "**Record**" includes—

(a) any document, manuscript and file;

(b) any microfilm, microfiche and facsimile copy of a document;

(c) any reproduction of image or images embodied in such microfilm (whether enlarged or not); and

(d) any other material produced by a computer or any other device;

(j) "**Right to information**" means the right to information accessible under this Act which is held by or under the control of any public authority and includes the right to—

(i) inspection of work, documents, records;

(ii) taking notes, extracts or certified copies of documents or records;

(iii) taking certified samples of material;

(iv) obtaining information in the form of diskettes, floppies, tapes, video cassettes or in any other electronic mode or through printouts where such information is stored in a computer or in any other device;

(k) "**State Information Commission**" means the State Information Commission constituted under sub-section (*1*) of section 15;

(l) "**State Chief Information Commissioner" and "State Information Commissioner**" mean the State Chief Information Commissioner and the State Information Commissioner appointed under sub-section (*3*) of section 15;

(m) "**State Public Information Officer**" means the State Public Information Officer designated under sub-section (*1*) and includes a State Assistant Public Information Officer designated as such under sub-section (*2*) of section 5;

(n) "**Third party**" means a person other than the citizen making a request for information and includes a public authority.

The main objectives of the RTI Act.—The soul objective of the Right to Information Act, 2005 is as following:

An Act to provide for setting out the practical regime of right to information for citizens to secure access to information under the control of public authorities, in order to promote transparency and accountability in the working of every public authority, the constitution of a Central Information Commission and State Information Commissions and for matters connected therewith or incidental thereto.

Above statement articulated as a soul objective in the Act includes the following objectives/points:

- **To set-up the practical regime**

  However, Article 19(1)(a) of the India's constitution provides "Freedom of Expression", as a Fundamental Right and as well as in the matter of *State of UP v. Raj Narain* (1975) 4 SCC 428,

Supreme Court of India has already declared "Right To Know" as a Fundamental Right under Article 19(1)(a). It means to know the information any one can approach to the High Court or Supreme Court directly, but this effort was not enough to avail the information properly and systematically as well as uncertainty was their regarding its applicability which was creating ambiguous situation and facing difficulties to avail the information from the various agencies of government and non-government organizations. Therefore, in order to provide systematic and concrete mechanism Parliament of India enacted "Right to Information Act, 2005" which facilitate the citizen to avail all kind of information with reasonable restriction mentioned as a general and specific exception under Sections 8, 9, and 24 of the same Act.

- **For citizens**
  According to Section 3 of RTI Act only citizen of India is eligible to file the application for any information subject to this Act but the guideline issued by Ministry of Personnel, Public Grievances and Pensions Department of Personnel and raining, through their letter No.1/69/2007-IR dated 27th February 2008, directs that, if any RTI Application filed on behalf of organization, in such case, instead of rejection that should be accepted as a personal application on behalf of that name of the person mentioned in the RTI Application.

- **To secure access to information under the control of public authorities**
  Definition of Public Authority articulated in Section 2(h) of RTI Act includes all the governmental organizations, and as well as, those Non-Governmental Organizations substantially financed by the Government but Act doesn't revealed the percentage of financial aids for this purpose which raise the ambiguous situation and dependability on the court's decision.
  The expression "under the control of public authority" which is perused in final part of the Section 2(f) while defining the word "Information" that, "information relating to any private body, which can be accessed by a public authority under any other law for the time being in force" means citizen can access the information which is directly related to the activities of that Public Authority as well as those information regarding private body which is held

by that Public authority. So in this way indirectly citizen can access the information related to the private bodies from the government offices who are authorised to control or monitor them, or connected in any way under any other laws for the time being in force.

- **To promote transparency and accountability in the working of every public authority**
  This Act ensure to eradicate any type of corruption in Public Authority by providing mandatory obligation to the Public Authority to make ensure to disseminate the information sought by the Indian citizen within a certain time period with nominal fee. As well as Section 4 impose Public authority to maintain and provide access all the information specified in the Section 4(b) by applying *suo motu* (self-initiative) action. So, due to the mandatory dissemination of information in the accessible format definitely transparency and accountability can established because that information not only help to aware the puple as well as could admit as a evidence in any legal procedure.

- **The constitution of a Central Information Commission and State Information Commissions**
  To provide the proper remedy with objectivity state and central commissions has been established separately by this Act (Refer Chapter 3 and 4 respectively). In such Commissions Second Appeal and Complaint can be filed by citizen without any fee. The status of Chief Commissioners and other Commissioners are same as the Chief and other Election Commissioners respectively.

- **Matters connected to Public Authority or incidental thereto**
  This is the first Act in India which provides the controlling power to the citizen in which Public Authorities are compelled to disseminate the information which is either directly or indirectly connected to them. Even if sought information is not belongs to particular Public Authority, in such case, that Public Authority is compelled to transfer to the relevant Public Authority instead of rejection.

  RTI is a necessary step taken to make our democracy work for the people in real sense. It goes without saying that an informed citizen is better equipped to keep necessary vigil on the instruments of governance and make the government more accountable to the governed. The Act is a big step towards making the citizens informed about the activities of the Government.

10.3 SCOPE AND EXTENT

1. This Act may be called the Right to Information Act, 2005.
2. It extends to the whole of India except the State of Jammu and Kashmir.
3. The provisions of sub-section (1) of section 4, sub-sections (1) and (2) of section 5, sections 12, 13, 15,16, 24, 27 and 28 shall come into force at once, and the remaining provisions of this Act shall come into force on the one hundred and twentieth day of its enactment.

10.4 RIGHT TO INFORMATION AND OBLIGATIONS OF PUBLIC AUTHORITIES

Subject to the provisions of this Act, all citizens shall have the right to information.

1. Every public authority shall—
   a. maintain all its records duly catalogued and indexed in a manner and the form which facilitates the right to information under this Act and ensure that all records that are appropriate to be computerised are, within a reasonable time and subject to availability of resources, computerised and connected through a network all over the country on different systems so that access to such records is facilitated;
   b. publish within one hundred and twenty days from the enactment of this Act,—
      i. the particulars of its organisation, functions and duties;
      ii. the powers and duties of its officers and employees;
      iii. the procedure followed in the decision-making process, including channels of supervision and accountability;
      iv. the norms set by it for the discharge of its functions;
      v. the rules, regulations, instructions, manuals and records, held by it or under its control or used by its employees for discharging its functions;

vi. a statement of the categories of documents that are held by it or under its control;

vii. the particulars of any arrangement that exists for consultation with, or representation by, the members of the public in relation to the formulation of its policy or implementation thereof;

viii. a statement of the boards, councils, committees and other bodies consisting of two or more persons constituted as its part or for the purpose of its advice, and as to whether meetings of those boards, councils, committees and other bodies are open to the public, or the minutes of such meetings are accessible for public;

ix. a directory of its officers and employees;

x. the monthly remuneration received by each of its officers and employees, including the system of compensation as provided in its regulations;

xi. the budget allocated to each of its agency, indicating the particulars of all plans, proposed expenditures and reports on disbursements made;

xii. the manner of execution of subsidy programmes, including the amounts allocated and the details of beneficiaries of such programmes;

xiii. particulars of recipients of concessions, permits or authorisations granted by it;

xiv. details in respect of the information, available to or held by it, reduced in an electronic form;

xv. the particulars of facilities available to citizens for obtaining information, including the working hours of a library or reading room, if maintained for public use;

xvi. the names, designations and other particulars of the Public Information Officers; and

xvii. such other information as may be prescribed and thereafter update these publications every year;

c. publish all relevant facts while formulating important policies or announcing the decisions which affect public; and

   d. provide reasons for its administrative or quasi-judicial decisions to affected persons.

2. It shall be a constant endeavour of every public authority to take steps in accordance with the requirements of clause (b) of sub-section (1) to provide as much information *suo motu* to the public at regular intervals through various means of communications, including internet, so that the public have minimum resort to the use of this Act to obtain information.
3. For the purposes of sub-section (1), every information shall be disseminated widely and in such form and manner which is easily accessible to the public.
4. All materials shall be disseminated taking into consideration the cost effectiveness, local language and the most effective method of communication in that local area and the information should be easily accessible, to the extent possible in electronic format with the Central Public Information Officer or State Public Information Officer, as the case may be, available free or at such cost of the medium or the print cost price as may be prescribed.

Explanation.—For the purposes of sub-sections (3) and (4), "disseminated" means making known or communicated the information to the public through notice boards, newspapers, public announcements, media broadcasts, the internet or any other means, including inspection of offices of any public authority

THE CENTRAL INFORMATION COMMISSION

1. The Central Government shall, by notification in the Official Gazette, constitute a body to be known as the Central Information Commission to exercise the powers conferred on, and to perform the functions assigned to it under this Act.
2. The Central Information Commission shall consist of—
   a. the Chief Information Commissioner; and
   b. such number of Central Information Commissioners, not exceeding ten, as may be deemed necessary.
3. The Chief Information Commissioner and Information Commissioners shall be appointed by the President on the recommendation of a committee consisting of—

i. the Prime Minister, who shall be the Chairperson of the committee;

ii. the Leader of Opposition in the Lok Sabha; and

iii. a Union Cabinet Minister to be nominated by the Prime Minister.

Explanation.—For the purposes of removal of doubts, it is hereby declared that where the Leader of Opposition in the House of the People has not been recognised as such, the Leader of the single largest group in opposition of the Government in the House of the People shall be deemed to be the Leader of Opposition.

4. The general superintendence, direction and management of the affairs of the Central Information Commission shall vest in the Chief Information Commissioner who shall be assisted by the Information Commissioners and may exercise all such powers and do all such acts and things which may be exercised or done by the Central Information Commission autonomously without being subjected to directions by any other authority under this Act.
5. The Chief Information Commissioner and Information Commissioners shall be persons of eminence in public life with wide knowledge and experience in law, science and technology, social service, management, journalism, mass media or administration and governance.
6. The Chief Information Commissioner or an Information Commissioner shall not be a Member of Parliament or Member of the Legislature of any State or Union territory, as the case may be, or hold any other office of profit or connected with any political party or carrying on any business or pursuing any profession.
7. The headquarters of the Central Information Commission shall be at Delhi and the Central Information Commission may, with the previous approval of the Central Government, establish offices at other places in India.

THE STATE INFORMATION COMMISSION

1. Every State Government shall, by notification in the Official Gazette, constitute a body to be known as the .... (name of the State) Information Commission to exercise the powers conferred on, and to perform the functions assigned to it under this Act.

2. The State Information Commission shall consist of—
   a. the State Chief Information Commissioner, and
   b. such number of State Information Commissioners, not exceeding ten, as may be deemed necessary.
3. The State Chief Information Commissioner and the State Information Commissioners shall be appointed by the Governor on the recommendation of a committee consisting of—
   i. the Chief Minister, who shall be the Chairperson of the committee;
   ii. the Leader of Opposition in the Legislative Assembly; and
   iii. a Cabinet Ministrer to be nominated by the Chief Minister.

   Explanation.—For the purposes of removal of doubts, it is hereby declared that where the Leader of Opposition in the Legislative Assembly has not been recognised as such, the Leader of the single largest group in opposition of the Government in the Legislative Assembly shall be deemed to be the Leader of Opposition.
4. The general superintendence, direction and management of the affairs of the State Information Commission shall vest in the State Chief Information Commissioner who shall be assisted by the State Information Commissioners and may exercise all such powers and do all such acts and things which may be exercised or done by the State Information Commission autonomously without being subjected to directions by any other authority under this Act.
5. The State Chief Information Commissioner and the State Information Commissioners shall be persons of eminence in public life with wide knowledge and experience in law, science and technology, social service, management, journalism, mass media or administration and governance.
6. The State Chief Information Commissioner or a State Information Commissioner shall not be a Member of Parliament or Member of the Legislature of any State or Union territory, as the case may be, or hold any other office of profit or connected with any political party or carrying on any business or pursuing any profession.
7. The headquarters of the State Information Commission shall be at such place in the State as the State Government may, by notification in the Official Gazette, specify and the State Information Commission may, with the previous approval of the State Government, establish offices at other places in the State.

10.5 POWERS AND FUNCTIONS OF THE INFORMATION COMMISSIONS, APPEAL AND PENALTIES

1. Subject to the provisions of this Act, it shall be the duty of the Central Information Commission or State Information Commission, as the case may be, to receive and inquire into a complaint from any person,—
   a. who has been unable to submit a request to a Central Public Information Officer or State Public Information Officer, as the case may be, either by reason that no such officer has been appointed under this Act, or because the Central Assistant Public Information Officer or State Assistant Public Information Officer, as the case may be, has refused to accept his or her application for information or appeal under this Act for forwarding the same to the Central Public Information Officer or State Public Information Officer or senior officer specified in sub-section (1) of section 19 or the Central Information Commission or the State Information Commission, as the case may be;
   b. who has been refused access to any information requested under this Act;
   c. who has not been given a response to a request for information or access to information within the time limit specified under this Act;
   d. who has been required to pay an amount of fee which he or she considers unreasonable;
   e. who believes that he or she has been given incomplete, misleading or false information under this Act; and
   f. in respect of any other matter relating to requesting or obtaining access to records under this Act.
2. Where the Central Information Commission or State Information Commission, as the case may be, is satisfied that there are reasonable grounds to inquire into the matter, it may initiate an inquiry in respect thereof.
3. The Central Information Commission or State Information Commission, as the case may be, shall, while inquiring into any matter under this section, have the same powers as are vested in a civil court while trying a suit under the Code of Civil Procedure, 1908, in respect of the following matters, namely:
   a. summoning and enforcing the attendance of persons and

compel them to give oral or written evidence on oath and to produce the documents or things;

b. requiring the discovery and inspection of documents;
c. receiving evidence on affidavit;
d. requisitioning any public record or copies thereof from any court or office;
e. issuing summons for examination of witnesses or documents; and
f. any other matter which may be prescribed.

4. Notwithstanding anything inconsistent contained in any other Act of Parliament or State Legislature, as the case may be, the Central Information Commission or the State Information Commission, as the case may be, may, during the inquiry of any complaint under this Act, examine any record to which this Act applies which is under the control of the public authority, and no such record may be withheld from it on any grounds.

19. 1. Any person who does not receive a decision within the time specified in sub-section (1) or clause (a) of sub-section (3) of section 7, or is aggrieved by a decision of the Central Public Information Officer or State Public Information Officer, as the case may be, may within thirty days from the expiry of such period or from the receipt of such a decision prefer an appeal to such officer who is senior in rank to the Central Public Information Officer or State Public Information Officer as the case may be, in each public authority:

Provided that such officer may admit the appeal after the expiry of the period of thirty days if he or she is satisfied that the appellant was prevented by sufficient cause from filing the appeal in time.

2. Where an appeal is preferred against an order made by a Central Public Information Officer or a State Public Information Officer, as the case may be, under section 11 to disclose third party information, the appeal by the concerned third party shall be made within thirty days from the date of the order.

3. A second appeal against the decision under sub-section (1) shall lie within ninety days from the date on which the decision should have been made or was actually received, with the Central Information Commission or the State Information Commission:

Provided that the Central Information Commission or the State Information Commission, as the case may be, may admit the appeal after the expiry of the period of ninety days if it is satisfied that the appellant was prevented by sufficient cause from filing the appeal in time.

4. If the decision of the Central Public Information Officer or State Public Information Officer, as the case may be, against which an appeal is preferred relates to information of a third party, the Central Information Commission or State Information Commission, as the case may be, shall give a reasonable opportunity of being heard to that third party.

5. In any appeal proceedings, the onus to prove that a denial of a request was justified shall be on the Central Public Information Officer or State Public Information Officer, as the case may be, who denied the request.

6. An appeal under sub-section (1) or sub-section (2) shall be disposed of within thirty days of the receipt of the appeal or within such extended period not exceeding a total of forty-five days from the date of filing thereof, as the case may be, for reasons to be recorded in writing.

7. The decision of the Central Information Commission or State Information Commission, as the case may be, shall be binding.

8. In its decision, the Central Information Commission or State Information Commission, as the case may be, has the power to—

a. require the public authority to take any such steps as may be necessary to secure compliance with the provisions of this Act, including—
    i. by providing access to information, if so requested, in a particular form;
    ii. by appointing a Central Public Information Officer or State Public Information Officer, as the case may be;
    iii. by publishing certain information or categories of information;
    iv. by making necessary changes to its practices in relation to the maintenance, management and destruction of records;
    v. by enhancing the provision of training on the right to information for its officials;
    vi. by providing it with an annual report in compliance with clause (b) of sub-section (1) of section 4;

b. require the public authority to compensate the complainant for any loss or other detriment suffered;
c. impose any of the penalties provided under this Act; and
d. reject the application.

9. The Central Information Commission or State Information Commission, as the case may be, shall give notice of its decision, including any right of appeal, to the complainant and the public authority.

10. The Central Information Commission or State Information Commission, as the case may be, shall decide the appeal in accordance with such procedure as may be prescribed.

20. 1. Where the Central Information Commission or the State Information Commission, as the case may be, at the time of deciding any complaint or appeal is of the opinion that the Central Public Information Officer or the State Public Information Officer, as the case may be, has, without any reasonable cause, refused to receive an application for information or has not furnished information within the time specified under sub-section (1) of section 7 or malafidely denied the request for information or knowingly given incorrect, incomplete or misleading information or destroyed information which was the subject of the request or obstructed in any manner in furnishing the information, it shall impose a penalty of two hundred and fifty rupees each day till application is received or information is furnished, so however, the total amount of such penalty shall not exceed twenty-five thousand rupees:

Provided that the Central Public Information Officer or the State Public Information Officer, as the case may be, shall be given a reasonable opportunity of being heard before any penalty is imposed on him:

Provided further that the burden of proving that he acted reasonably and diligently shall be on the Central Public Information Officer or the State Public Information Officer, as the case may be.

2. Where the Central Information Commission or the State Information Commission, as the case may be, at the time of deciding any complaint or appeal is of the opinion that the Central Public Information Officer or the State Public Information Officer, as the

case may be, has, without any reasonable cause and persistently, failed to receive an application for information or has not furnished information within the time specified under sub-section (1) of section 7 or malafidely denied the request for information or knowingly given incorrect, incomplete or misleading information or destroyed information which was the subject of the request or obstructed in any manner in furnishing the information, it shall recommend for disciplinary action against the Central Public Information Officer or the State Public Information Officer, as the case may be, under the service rules applicable to him.

10.6 CONCLUSION

- The Right to Information Act will become operational by the 12th October 2005.
- The objective of the Act is to provide for setting out the practical regime of right to information for citizens to secure access to information under the control of public authorities, in order to promote transparency and accountability in the working of every public authority, the constitution of a Central Information Commission and State Information Commissions and for matters connected therewith or incidental thereto.
- There are two levels of information commission:
    - Central Information Commission
    - State Information Commission

TEST QUESTIONS

1. What do you understand by term Information Technology? Explain the rationale behind the Information Technology Act, 2000.
2. Explain the term "e-commerce" and "e-governance" with reference to Information Technology Act, 2000.
3. What are the objectives of Cyber Laws? Explain.
4. Define the following terms as used in the Information Technology Act, 2000:
   (i) Digital signature; (ii) Asymmetric crypto system; (iii) Electronic record; (iv) Private key and Public key; (v) Computer network; (vi) Originator; (vii) Computer Database; (vii) Computer virus.
5. How is "Controller of Certifying Authorities" appointed? What

are his functions under the Information Technology Act, 2000?

6. Discuss the power of "Controller of Certifying Authorities" under the Information Technology Act, 2000.
7. Discuss the duties of "Certifying Authorities" under the Information Technology Act, 2000.
8. Discuss the provisions of Information Technology Act, 2000 relating to "Digital Signature Certificate".
9. Enumerate the activities relating to computer, computer network, etc. which are subject to sanction and penalized, if indulged without the permission of the owner or the person-in-charge.
10. How is "Cyber Appellate Tribunal" established? What are its powers under the Information Technology Act, 2000? Discuss.
11. Discuss the provision of Information Technology Act, 2000 relating to appointment, term of office, salary, resignation and removal of the Presiding Officer of the Cyber Appellate Tribunal.

BIBLIOGRAPHY

Fabio Bortolotti, Remedies Available to thc Sctller and Seller's Right to Require Specific Performance (Articles 61, 62 and 28), 25 J.L. & Com. 335 (2005).

Furmston M.P. and Cheshire G.C., 2012. *Cheshire, Fifoot and Furmston's Law of Contract*, Oxford: Oxford University Press.

Hannigan B., 2012. *Company Law*, Oxford: Oxford University Press.

Jones, Lucy, 2013a. *Introduction to Business Law*, Oxford: Oxford University Press.

Jones, Lucy, 2013b. *Introduction to Business Law*, Oxford: Oxford University Press.

Law J. & Martin E.A. eds., 2013. *A Dictionary of Law*, Oxford: Oxford University Press.

Law, Jonathan, 2009. *A Dictionary of Law [e-book]*, Available at: https://catalogue.kent.ac.uk/Record/996959.

MacIntyre E., 2013. *Essentials of Business Law with My Law Chamber Premium Pack*, Harlow: Pearson/Education.

Marson J., 2013. *Business Law*, © 2013: Oxford University Press. Available at: http://capitadiscovery.co.uk/medway-ac/items/744884?query=Business+Law+marson&resultsUri= items%3Fquery%3DBusiness%2BLaw%2Bmarson.

Marson, James, *Business Law*, Oxford: Oxford University Press.

Poole J., 2014. *Casebook on Contract Law*, Oxford: Oxford University Press.

R.C. Hoeber, *Contemporary Business Law* (1982).

Riches S., 2013. *Keenan and Riches' Business law*, Harlow, England: Pearson/Education. Available at: https://www.dawsonera.com/guard/protected/dawson.jsp?name=https://sid.kent.ac.uk/

shibboleth&dest=http://www.dawsonera.com/depp/reader/protected/external/AbstractView/S9781447922940.

Riches, Sarah, Allen, Vida, and Keenan, Denis J., 2013. *Keenan and Riches' Business Law*, Harlow: Longman. Available at: http://lib.myilibrary.com/?id=502451&entityid=https://oala.surrey.ac.uk/oala/metada

Taylor R.D. and Taylor D., 2011. *Contract Law*, Oxford: Oxford University Press.

Thomas S. Atkin and Lloyd M. Rinehart, The Effect of Negotiation Practices on the Relationship Between Suppliers and Customers, 22 Negotiation J. 47 (2006).

Turner C., 2014. *Unlocking Contract Law*, London: Routledge.

Web Portal

www.slideshare.net/.../negotiable-instruments-act-1881-14696589
cab.org.in › Knowledge Bank
en.wikipedia.org/wiki/Negotiable_Instruments_Act,_1881
www.ncdrc.nic.in/1_1.html
consumeraffairs.nic.in/l
awcommissionofindia.nic.in/1-50/report8.pdf
www.bclaws.ca/civix/document/id/complete/statreg/96410_01
www.lawnotes.in › Home › Indian Law › Indian Acts
en.wikipedia.org/wiki/Indian_Contract_Act_1872

INDEX

Acceptor and Drawee Liability, 34
Acceptor for Honour, 31
Access, means, 86
Account Closed, 63
Addressee, means, 95
Adjudicating Officer, means, 95
Affixing Digital Signature, means, 95
Ambiguous Instruments, 24
Appeals, 135
Application for Licence, 96
Appointment of Controller, 94
Appointment of Officers and their Powers and Function, 154
Appropriate Government, means, 95, 164
Appropriate Laboratory, means, 114
Assignment, 68
Asymmetric Crypto System, means, 86, 88

Banker's draft, 26
Bearer Instrument, 25
Bearer, 42
Bill of Exchange and Promissory Note
  Difference Between, 15
Bill of Exchange, 12
  Essential Features, 12
  Procedure for Transfer, 13
Branch office, means, 116

Central Information Commission, means, 164
Central Public Information Officer, means, 164
Certification practice statement, means, 95
Certifying Authority, means, 95
Cheque and a Bill of Exchange
  Difference Between, 22
Cheque, 14
  Dishonour of, 17
  Essential Features, 14
Competent Authority, means, 164
Complainant, means, 116
Complaint, means, 116
Composition of the State Commission, 131
Computer Network, means, 96
Computer Resource, means, 96
Computer System, means, 96
Computer, means, 96
Consequences of not giving Notice of Dishonour, 60
Consideration, 40
Consumer Dispute, means, 117
Consumer Protection Act, 1986, 112-48
  Appeal, 140
  Composition of the District Forum, 125
  Composition of the National Commission, 136
  Composition of the State Commission, 131
  Consumer Disputes Redressal Agencies, 124

Consumer Protection Councils, 122
Consumer Rights, 113
Penalties, 142-43
Consumer, means, 116
Controller to Act as Repository, 96
Controller, means, 96
Conversion, 36
Cyber Appellate Tribunal, means, 96

Darshani Hundi, 6
Data, means, 96
Defect, means, 117
Defective Title, 42
Deficiency, means, 117
Demand instrument, 6
Digital Signature Certificate, means, 88
Digital Signature, means, 87
Discharge by Operation of Law is not Included, 52
Discharge by Operation of Law, 52
Discharge of Indorser Liability, 35
Discharge of Negotiable Instruments, 48
Discharge of Parties from Liability, 51
Discharge of Party Secondarily Liable, 49
Discharge, means, 47
Dishonour of Negotiable Instrument, 58
District Forum, means, 117
Documentery Bill, 26
Drawee in Case of Need, 31

Effect of Dishonour, 58
Effect of other Endorsements, 64
Electronic Form, means, 88
Electronic Gazette, means, 88
Electronic Record, means, 88
Endorsement, 69
Environmental Laboratories, 159
Environmental Pollutant, means, 150
Environmental pollution, means, 151

Fictitious Bill, 26
Fictitious Payee Rule, 36
Filing a Complaint with State Commission, 134
Finding of the District Forum, 129
Foreign Instrument, 24
Fraudulent Endorsements by Employees, 36
Functions of Controller, 94
Furnishing of Information to Authorities and Agencies, 156

General Crossing, 16
Goods, means, 117
Government Analysts, 159

Hazardous Substance, means, 154
Hearing of Appeal, 135
Holder and Holder in Due Course Difference between, 41
Holder and Holder in Due Course, 36
Holder for Value, 41
Holder means, 36

Imposter Rule, 36
Inchoate Stamped Instruments, 24
Indorser Liability, 34
Information, means, 88, 165
Inland Instrument, 24
Instruments Payable on Demand, 24
Intermediary, means, 88

Jurisdiction of the District Forum, 127
Jurisdiction of the National Commission, 138
Jurisdiction of the State Commission, 134

Key pair, means, 88

Liability of Parties, 32
Liability of Prior Parties to Holder in Due Course, 42
Liability of the Drawer, 42

Manufacturer, means, 117
Member, means, 117
Mistake in Payment or Acceptance, 35
Modes of Negotiation, 68
Muddati Hundi, 6

National Commission, means, 117
Negligence, 36
Negotiable Instruments Act, 1881, Section 4, 10
Negotiable Instruments
Parties to, 30
Negotiable Instruments
Types of, 24
Negotiable Instruments, 1-8
Negotiation Back, 74
Negotiation, 67
Not a Clearing Member, 64
Notice of Dishonour, 58
Notification, means, 118

Offences by Companies, 160
Offences by Government Departments, 161
Order Instrument, 24

Payable to Bearer, 20
Payable to Order, 20
Payment in Due Course, 41
Penalty for Contravention, 160
Person, means, 118
Persons Handling Hazardous Substances, 156
Possession, 42
Power to give Directions, 154
Power to take Sample and Procedure, 158
Powers and Functions of the Information Commissions, Appeal and Penalties, 174
Powers of Entry and Inspection, 156
Powers Provided by the Act to Central Government, 152
Prescribed, means, 118, 154, 165
Presentment of a Draft or Check, 35
Presentment of a Note, 35
Prevention, Control, and Abatement of Environmental Pollution, 155
Primary vs. Secondary Liability, 34
Privileges of Holder in Due Course, 38
Promissory Note, Essential features, 11
Public Authority, means, 165

Quasi Negotiable Instruments, 6

Recognition of foreign Certifying Authorities, 95
Record, means, 165
Refer to Drawer, 64
Regulation, means, 118
Renewal of Licence, 97
Reports of Government Analysts, 159
Restrictive Trade Practice, means, 118
Right to Information Act, 2005, 163-78
Right to Information and Obligations of Public Authorities, 169
Right to Information, means, 165
Rules Regarding Accommodation Bills, 25
Rules to Regulate Environmental Pollution, 155

Scope and Extent, 169
Secure Digital Signature, 93
Secure Electronic Record, 93
Security Procedure, 94
Service, means, 118
Shah-jog Hundi, 5
Signing an Instrument, 35
Special Crossing, 16
Spurious Goods and Services, means, 118
State Commission, means, 119
State Information Commission, means, 166
State Public Information Officer, means, 166
Stop Payment, Instructions, 63

The Acceptor, means, 31
The Drawee, means, 30, 32
The Drawer, means, 30
The Endorsee, means, 31, 32
The Endorser, means, 31, 32
The Environment (Protection) Act, 1986, 149-62
The Holder, means, 31, 32
The Information Technology Act, 2008, 84-111

Attribution, Acknowledgment and Despatch of Electronic Records, 91
Cyber Regulations Appellate Tribunal, 106
Digital Signature Certificates, 100
Digital Signature, 88-89
Duties of Subscribers, 102
Electronic Governance, 89
Penalties and Adjudication, 104
Prevention of Fraud, 109
Regulation of Certifying Authorities, 94
Secure Electronic Records and Secure Digital Signatures, 93
The Maker, means, 31
The Payee, means, 31, 32
Third Party, means, 166
Time Instrument, 6
Trader, means, 119
Transfer of Cases, 134

Undated bills, 26
Unfair Trade Practice, means, 119

Warranty Liability, 35